Make
your own good
Fortune

Make
your own good
Fortune

HOW TO SEIZE
LIFE'S OPPORTUNITIES

DOUGLAS MILLER

ESSENTIAL STEPS TO TRANSFORMING YOUR LIFE

Educational Publishers LLP trading as BBC Active
Edinburgh Gate
Harlow
Essex CM20 2JE
England

First published 2006

ISBN: 0 563 52003 5

Commissioning Editor: Emma Shackleton
Project Editor: Jeanette Payne
Copy Editor: Christine King
Designer: Kevin O'Connor
Senior Production Controller: Man Fai Lau

Printed and bound by Ashford Colour Press Ltd, UK

The Publisher's policy is to use paper manufactured from sustainable forests.

'2B or not 2B' is reproduced courtesy of Spike Milligan Productions Limited.

Contents

At the end of my life I want still to be standing up rather than on my knees. To say that I stood up to the world and had a go rather than letting all the opportunities I had slip through my hands.

Introduction
The higher the wall – the bigger the sky

- ❏ Your original soundtrack

- ❏ Born free

- ❏ What's an opportunity?

- ❏ Where do you think you're going?

- ❏ Opportunities exist everywhere

- ❏ Life-defining moments

- ❏ Survive and then thrive

On a recent flight from central Europe to London's Gatwick Airport, I looked out of the window on a brilliantly clear night. As far as I could see was a vast spread of lights (some still, some moving), silver rivers, mountain ranges and other aeroplanes all apparently mixed together as though a mirror had reflected everything about life itself back to me. It's a sight many of us will be familiar with and, unless you're a terrified flier, most of us never seem to tire of the possibilities that exist in what we see. We begin to imagine what some of the people below might be doing. Working, having a drink, playing sport, listening to music, arguing, driving, sailing in a ship on the sea, being a child or maybe making love. Humanity perhaps expressing itself to humanity at its best and worst and continually creating new things out of old.

As I looked out of the window, I had one of those enlightened moments where I was able to feel proud to be part of the never-ending explosion of opportunity that life is able to offer us. Many readers will have had similar experiences. A groundswell of excitement builds in us as we recognize what is there – we maybe see a beauty in the multi-faceted world of which we are a part and which is less apparent when we are on the ground.

Of course in that short time in the aeroplane everything becomes a little clearer. The hard part is that from the aeroplane we are able to see this panorama of energy, excitement and opportunity laid out before us but we cannot access it. It is untouchable. Give me a parachute, you might say, and then I can land in the middle of it and absorb myself in everything that's around me. But when we arrive at the airport those feelings have subsided, as we deal with the mundane details of collecting luggage, joining the back of a huge passport queue and negotiating the final stage of the journey.

Imagine now that you don't come from one of the world's richer countries (and maybe you don't).

A seminal film, *Kandahar*, charts a young woman's passage across Iran and Afghanistan as she tries to reach her suicidal sister in Kandahar. The young woman (who is Afghani but lives in Canada) comes across a seemingly endless world of suppression, petty thieving and futility. And yet even in that brutalizing environment one young man is able to utter an expression of wonderful optimism: 'When the walls are high, the sky is even higher.'

The frustrations of living behind a huge wall separating us from opportunity makes the limitlessness of the sky (of opportunity) all the more obvious because we cannot touch it.

For Afghanis the walls are very real and very large. But how big and how real are the barriers, the walls, that are placed in front of our own lives?

Like my experience in the aeroplane, those who come from poorer parts of the world can see the opportunities that exist elsewhere but are very difficult to access. In wealthier countries we are remarkably lucky to have what we have. But we often choose to position ourselves in the metaphorical aeroplane – looking, but not realizing that we have a parachute available that can land us right in the middle of it. We find all kinds of reasons not to make the most of what is there for us, and later regret that we didn't take the chances we had.

■ Your original soundtrack

This is a book about Spotting (and Taking) Opportunities. However, it may get rather tedious for you the reader to see the words 'Opportunity Spotting and Taking' in almost every paragraph. So from here on in we will abbreviate 'Opportunity Spotting and Taking' (and Spotters and Takers) to a more simple OST – with occasional reminders as to what this refers to.

Lovers of film and film music will also recognize OST as an abbreviation of 'original soundtrack'. If you value diversity in your life and recognize that you are different from everybody else, then you will be keen to play out your life as an 'original soundtrack' – as an expression of your individuality, your personality and above all of your capabilities. It is a characteristic of OSTs that they want to express themselves to the world – they want to bring some originality to it through their thoughts (Opportunity Spotters) and/or through their actions (Opportunity Takers). This desire to play your life as though it were an original soundtrack provides a prime motivation to be an OST.

As the quote on page 8 suggests, it can be a powerful exercise to imagine yourself at the end of your life, reflecting back on it, thinking what you would like to say about it – notwithstanding the fact that you may be nowhere near the end of it! Those who can stand up to the world and say they had a go are likely to be the ones who decided to pluck at the fruit of the opportunity tree during their lifetime. Those who live with regrets based in their own mental and physical inertia are likely to be the ones who let the fruit rot or who didn't even look up to see what was available for picking.

So when the soundtrack of your life is played at the end of it, do you want it to be an original one? Do you want to say 'If only' or do you want to say 'I gave it my best shot'? It really is down to you.

■ Born free

> *I was free. I was affronted by freedom. The day's silence said, 'Go where you will. It's all yours. You asked for it. It's up to you now. You're on your own and nobody's going to stop you.'*

Laurie Lee, *As I Walked Out One Midsummer Morning*

Laurie Lee experienced this feeling as he left home to walk to London and then on to Spain. His great books are being slowly forgotten by newer generations as he describes a Europe few will believe existed so recently (the 1930s). What Lee expresses so beautifully in his writing is the complete sense of mental and physical freedom he has as he explores (for him) new worlds. The first step we take to be an OST is to recognize the freedom we have to think in whatever ways we wish. And in societies that champion freedom we also have the freedom to express those thoughts to the outside world.

For almost all 18-year-olds this sense of opening one's arms to the world should be so strong that it is almost instinctive – and yet at such a vibrant age there are many who are already building the wall that will stop the search and experimentation that is so important in the formative years. As we advance in age, we can also observe people in apparently similar circumstances who clearly have differing views about the opportunities available to them. Two examples include single parenthood and retirement.

No one would question that single parenthood is tough. And yet there are plenty of single parents searching out and taking opportunities, even when money is very short, while others aren't even trying to see what the possibilities are. Perhaps it is a simple question of growing a mindset that concentrates on what we can do rather than what we cannot. It works the same way in retirement. Exercising the mental muscle is critical at any age but particularly so in the third age, as Ann's story demonstrates later in this book (pages 128–130). Her story helps to reaffirm the belief that never-ending opportunities can exist no matter what stage of our life we have reached.

So why is it that if we look at people living in seemingly tough circumstances, we see some of them apparently paralysed by their circumstances (real or imagined) while others are getting on with a life full of Opportunity Spotting? Clearly some of us have nurtured the 'Can Do' mindset while others get locked into a 'Can't Do' existence.

■ What's an opportunity?

So what do we mean by opportunities? When I suggested to friends that I was writing a book on Spotting Opportunities, almost everyone assumed that it would be aimed at the business reader to help them spot business opportunities for themselves or for organizations looking to develop new products, services and markets. Those angles are of course essential in forward-looking, democratic societies because they are manifestations of our need as human beings to be curious, to explore and to create, out of our own imaginations and/or those of others, opportunity. It is also clear that as we spend a substantial part of our lives at work (or, if you truly engage with your job, 'at play'), this should provide an obvious arena for OSTs. Even within our daytime occupation, massive opportunities exist for the entrepreneur seeking to play out the dream of having a business for real; the intrapreneur seeking to advance his or her career within the workplace; the searcher looking for a new job opportunity; and the self-employed person working out ways of selling themselves to new clients and markets.

Clearly our earning occupation takes up a significant part of our day, but there are many other situations where spotting and taking opportunities provide the bedrock for a more fulfilling life. Retirement activities, bringing up children, creative use of leisure time in the evening and at weekends – all provide us with abundant opportunities if we decide to look for them. Opportunity Spotting is integral to human progress on a global scale and integral to personal fulfilment on a personal one.

The great thing is that our opportunities can come from almost anywhere. We often assume that opportunities come to us from the world around us. More often than not, however, they are conceived and born within our rich and varied imaginations – though we do need to connect with our inner world to find them.

One dictionary definition says that opportunities present 'the possibility of doing something'. These five words – the possibility of doing something – neatly define the psychology behind opportunities. Opportunities are only ever possibilities – they are never absolute. The difficulty here for many people is that they wait for the opportunity to become a certainty. We like to have all the information available to us that proves that the opportunity is the absolute certainty we want. We gain our security from what we believe to be the truth. But no opportunity is absolute. Perfect information does not exist. We risk the danger of opportunity paralysis because we want to know that the coast is clear before we venture out. The more we have to lose, the less we are inclined to risk it. Perhaps this explains why those with little to lose are ready to go for it if the chink of light is shown to them. The challenge for us as opportunity spotters in affluent societies is to risk a part of what we have for the possibility, rather than the certainty, of something better or different.

■ Where do you think you're going?

Life's too short to be just passing through.
Carr Hagerman, *motivational story-teller*

As fewer and fewer of us believe in life after death, we may want to live some kind of life before death! And even if we believe we are just 'passing through' on our way to somewhere else, that doesn't mean that we should stop 'living' because this is just a small fragment of an eternal existence.

Being aware of our own mortality can often create the fire inside that pushes us on to maximize the time that's left for us. Taking our very existence for granted means we become inclined to abuse that most precious thing: time. If you have a god then life presents an opportunity to prepare yourself for the next world. Non-believers (and I am one) may not understand or believe in the idea of another world, but I contend later in this book that as well as coming in all shapes and sizes we also come with six billion worlds attached – the worlds of our fellow inhabitants. If we spend our time questioning the lives of everyone else, it probably means that we are not doing very much with our own. Think about the opportunities that your life offers for you, rather than worrying about how other people choose to live theirs.

Celebrating our individual existence and all that it holds for us means that when we get nearer the end than the beginning of it, we can hold our head up and say, 'I had a go.'

■ Opportunities exist everywhere

Here's a lateral look at what spotting opportunities can mean. I was working with a group of housing workers from Birmingham City Council in the UK (Europe's largest local authority), and I was talking about how we spend eight hours a day at work for most of our lives and how important it is therefore that we at least try to enjoy as much of it as we can. I followed that up by saying that we also have eight hours a day for leisure and the same applies here too – try and make the most of it. At this point a sharp-thinking participant (by the name of Anthony Quinn – thanks, Anthony) said, 'That also means that we spend eight hours of each day in bed. That means you should spend a bit more on a good bed.' The logic was brilliant. We have the *opportunity* to have a better night's sleep if we want it. Why not take it?

Can I pause for breath sometimes?

But now for a bit of healthy contradiction! An Indian philosopher once said, 'We spend much of our time being human doings and have forgotten to be human beings.' We often, particularly in the most 'advanced' societies, assume a limited interpretation of what spotting and taking opportunities can really mean. Does taking an opportunity always need to involve large amounts of activity? Of course not! It can mean a picnic in the country or reading a book in quiet surroundings. It can mean watching the sunset or gazing at the stars. In fact, if you're looking for the great business opportunity or an answer to a problem that needs solving, taking time out to 'smell the roses' can often freshen up the mind so that it can create the ideas and possibilities for the bigger opportunities. Thinking too hard can be counter-productive.

In the 1920s the leader of the British coal miners' union, A. J. Cook, came up with the demand for eight hours for work, eight hours for sleep and 'eight hours for own repose'. People were very conscious, even nearly a hundred years ago, of the need for relaxation, and sometimes we need to draw ourselves away from the pressure now placed on us by society to be constantly on the move. A life of relentless opportunity spotting can be as one-dimensional as a life in the armchair.

■ Life-defining moments

We can all, if we pause to think about it for just a few seconds, produce a list of life-defining moments (LDMs) that have altered the direction our life was taking or produced a fundamental change in the way we saw our world. You may find it useful to think about your list now – there may be moments of euphoria at one extreme to the less pleasant aspects of being a human being at the other. Your list could include school experiences, special relationships, job changes and marriage through to illness and possibly bereavement. There will be things on your list that you share with many other people. However, what makes each list unique, and you as well, is that you are likely to include a combination of experiences or LDMs that are unlike anybody else's.

There are two ways of looking at these LDMs. Some will be events over which we had little personal control, and often hadn't personally planned for – redundancy, for example. Overcoming these difficulties will require all the traits of Positive Thinking for which I hope the companion book to this, *Positive Thinking, Positive Action*, will provide some help.

However, as we examine our list of LDMs we may also see a pattern emerge with a number of them. Many will be moments where we chose to take an action, to grasp an opportunity through our own proactive approach. Identify these on your list with a simple 'P' for 'proactive'. A second pattern is that we will have a number of LDMs where 'the world happened to us' – events such as redundancy as mentioned previously. Put a little 'R' by those that were reactive. It is very difficult to comment on personal lists without appearing to make harsh judgements on the way we live our lives. But this book is about realism (a theme developed in Part One) and perhaps those judgements need to be made. So if, for example, your list contains very few LDMs where you *proactively* decided to make the action that provoked them, then you may be guilty of not seeking opportunity and challenge. And if in addition to this you have a substantial number of reactive LDMs, then you may be guilty of reacting to circumstances, of letting circumstances control you. There is nothing wrong with a large number of reactive LDMs because it is extremely difficult to predict when they will happen. The difficulty for potential opportunity spotters occurs when we have a high number of reactive LDMs and a low number of proactive LDMs.

Have a look at your personal list and ask how many of these LDMs came from your own proactive approach to your world. Did you join a club? Did you take up a new hobby? Did you change jobs? Did you travel? Did you take on more responsibility? Did you enter a competition? Did you ask that person out to dinner? Did you start a family? Proactive opportunity takers try to do one or both of these:

1 When we proactively create opportunities, we seek to exercise the mental muscle by thinking about present and future possibilities when there is no immediate or obvious pressure to do so.

2 Alternatively we may proactively take opportunities where others have applied new thinking to a situation but where we now take up the reins and put this new thinking into practice.

Imagine yourself with your arms stretched out in front of you but with your hands tightly clasped together. In this position we are shutting off the opportunities of the world because we are putting a barrier between those same opportunities and ourselves. The proactive OSTs have their arms stretched wide out as though we were going to hug or embrace someone. We seek to embrace our world rather than position something between ourselves and the possibilities our world represents for us. Proactive OSTs seek to embrace their own ideas and those of other people.

Reactive OSTs show many of the character traits of the proactive opportunity takers but with one key difference. The proactive OSTs are taking an 'I can happen to life' approach, whereas the reactive OSTs may say, 'I let life happen to me.' Of course, we all have to be reactive some of the time – reality dictates that there will always be an unplanned-for event. A little forward thinking can help here. By asking ourselves what we would do if we were, for example, made redundant, or forced to move home, we have already mentally prepared ourselves to some extent for the necessary mindset. And the mindset needs to be a positive one. Out of the big problem a big opportunity can be born – it just depends on how we react to that problem. Where we take the chance to change direction. In many cases these unplanned-for events can be made to be the best things that ever happened to us.

■ Survive and then thrive

Can it be true? Can we see opportunity in the toughest of circumstances? Can we see opportunity where others are just trying to survive? It is possible.

Earlier, I said that in any situation we always have the freedom to think in whatever way we so choose. It is also worth remembering that in any given situation, no matter how grave, we can always choose our response to it as a result of that 'free-thinking'. The artist Ronald Searle recalled how being in a Japanese prisoner of war camp challenged the very core of his psyche. He found refuge in his drawings, trading what he could for paper and drawing implements. He told himself that he would get out along with all the drawings he had produced while he was imprisoned – many of which depicted the full horrors of the camp.

Ronald Searle managed to see an opportunity in horrendous circumstances – he found a way to continue with his passion and also use it as a vehicle for optimism. He created a reason to survive because he was able to develop a sense that he would have a future where his passion would be a part of that future. He could see the end of the tunnel even if the tunnel was a very long one. Many readers now will know him as the creator of the highly popular *St Trinian's* cartoons.

Free 'Thinking'

'Thinking' is your best friend. But Thinking has had a few problems in life and has ended up in prison. All the different experiences, knockbacks, discouraging parental care, failures and disappointments meant that Thinking struggled to see things in the way it did when it was very young. Thinking found that it was harder to exercise itself when it got older. So Thinking built a wall, so thick that even the toughest parts of life experiences couldn't get through. Thinking's prison now has four big walls so high and strong that no one can get in. The problem is that Thinking can't get out either. Thinking felt very safe but life was very dull. Nothing ever seemed to happen to Thinking.

Fortunately help was at hand. Thinking had some mental tools available that would help it knock the wall down. Thinking found that some of the small tools were useful in making initial inroads into the wall itself. But sometimes a big sledgehammer was needed to knock over the biggest bricks. Thinking found that it wasn't necessary to knock down all the bricks. That would be a waste of effort. It was necessary to knock down only those bricks that were preventing escape. Eventually, with some hard work along the way, Thinking was able to escape from the prison.

Would Thinking go back to prison? Well, those old influences don't go away and sometimes Thinking can find the bricks building up around it. But Thinking knows how to knock the bricks down now.

Not only is your friend Thinking out of jail – you haven't even had to pay a ransom! Thinking is now free. And so is Thinking's capacity to spot and take opportunities.

OK, I'm thinking. Where to now?

This book is divided into two distinct parts that help us to both spot and take opportunities. Part One provides a clear 'road map', a step-by-step process that begins with the spotting of opportunities and ends when we go to live with the opportunity – where it moves from the imagination to the real world. Part Two does two things. It provides 12 opportunity tools (the Opportunity Taker's Tool-kit) that will help us work better with the opportunities that exist for us by providing a range of mindsets and thought processes that will help us as OSTs and it gives real stories of people who sought successfully to inject some opportunity spotting and taking into their own lives.

Opportunity spotting and taking – it's the difference between going through life with your eyes wide open, or choosing to hide in a cave when the sun comes out.

Part One
The road map – from opportunity to action

- ❏ Stage 1(a) The search engine
- ❏ Stage 1(b) Incompatibility
- ❏ Stage 2 The download
- ❏ Stage 3 Filtering
- ❏ Stage 4 You are connected!

If we pause to think about our lives up to now, we see how often the key moments are based either in our reaction to things that have happened to us, or in our capacity to anticipate the things that we think might happen. In other words, where we either react to events, or where we try to anticipate the future and proactively develop a plan to make the most of what we perceive to be the future. In Part Two we will look at a series of mindsets, action points and case studies to help us both spot and take opportunities. At this stage it can be useful to have some sort of mental road map that will take us from the purest form of opportunity spotting – where we create an opportunity at the point where there may be no obvious need to – right through to 'going live' with the decisions we make about our opportunities. One that moves us on from the setting of a personal goal through to the actions required to bring our goal to life.

When we identify a goal for ourselves we will either have developed it through the necessity to solve some kind of problem (redundancy, for example) or because we have seen, without any necessity to see or seek it, an opportunity (a business opportunity, for example). As we have seen already in this book, the solution to an existing problem can often create a new exciting opportunity for us anyway.

But what happens next? As we introduce the idea of more committed opportunity search into our lives, we can find ourselves having wonderful thoughts (where we generate ideas to help make the most of our opportunity or solve the problem we have) but we struggle to sharpen our thinking at the critical point so that we can successfully run with the best ideas we have. It is at this stage that we need good decision-making skills. Once we have made a decision as to which idea we are going to run with, we then move into the all-important action phase where we 'go live' with the solution we have generated. So the process I have described in the last few paragraphs is as follows:

Spot the opportunity OR identify a problem
THEN

Work out some possible ways of making the most of the
opportunity or solving the problem
THEN

Select a solution
THEN

'Go live' with the solution

There are many models rich in metaphor that help us to understand the psychology required to carry us through this process. For myself, I favour contemporary computer language because the image the language creates in my mind neatly demonstrates the thinking behind each of the stages: the Search Engine or Incompatibility, the Download, Filtering, and You are Connected! I have also borrowed from the inspirational writer on creative thinking, Roger von Oech, because his metaphors juxtapose my own. He uses different 'roles' to illustrate the stages we work through:

Explorer (Search Engine)

Artist (Download)

Judge (Filtering)

Warrior (You Are Connected!)

I've added another, between Explorer and Artist: Doctor (Incompatibility).

For those readers who prefer a visual depiction of what has been said already in this section, the following chart summarizes the stages and the computer metaphors (mine) and the 'roles' (all but one Roger von Oech's) behind each of these stages. You may want to familiarize yourself with this chart anyway because it is the backbone for much of this chapter and provides a useful 'at a glance' reference as you read on.

		Roger von Oech's 'roles'	Computer analogies
Stage 1(a) OR	Spotting opportunities	Explorer	The search engine
Stage 1(b) Out of which comes a goal THEN	What is the problem?	Doctor [my addition]	Incompatibility
Stage 2	Possible solutions	Artist	The download
Stage 3	Making right decisions	Judge	Filtering
Stage 4	Going live	Warrior	You are connected!
GOAL			

◼ The opportunity curve

Futurologist Joel Barker has also provided some helpful tools in highlighting the dangers of the reactive approach and the benefits in acting early to change your circumstances before the circumstances come and change you.

Take a look at the opportunity curve opposite – it presents the reality of living for many of us. The curve is divided into four parts: A, B, C and D. There are two axes: stimulation on the vertical and time on the horizontal.

Phase A represents that time when you are looking for a new opportunity. The line stays horizontal because you haven't yet taken one up. The opportunity could relate to almost any situation:

- New business start-up
- Third-agers looking for retirement possibilities
- Education
- Employment opportunities
- Large corporations searching for new products or services
- Life itself!

The opportunity curve

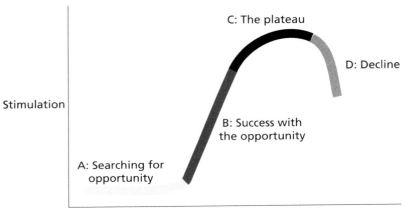

Perhaps we are searching because we have a problem that needs a solution (redundancy or dissatisfaction with our current job), or perhaps our opportunity is of a more freeform kind (the recognition that we all need new stimuli). At the end of Phase A we have pitched ourselves into the new opportunity and, with a mixture of emotions – excitement, fear, curiosity, nervousness – we move into Phase B of the opportunity curve.

Phase B is the success phase. Things are going well for us and the curve moves upwards. The shape of the curve will vary. Some of us will meet success quickly with our new opportunity (with the curve therefore steeper). For some it may take time (with a flatter curve). And of course others will go straight back to Phase A (or give up on opportunities altogether) because they haven't met the desired success with the new opportunity.

But here is the danger! The time of success is also a time of weakness. Things are going well for us, and so we fail to notice that things may need to change. But why should we? Things are going fine the way they are – or so we think. Imagine you have a successful small business. Others will have noticed the formula you use – you have written the blueprint for them, remember – and will copy and improve on it. Or come up with an innovation that you hadn't seen. Consider some of the world's largest airlines that grew exponentially in the 1980s and early 1990s. Suddenly airlines like South West Airlines and JetBlue in the USA and Ryanair and easyJet in Europe changed the whole model for the way we buy flight tickets, and the big airlines started to struggle to compete on shorter routes. We look at the innovative mindset of some of these low-cost carriers later on in the book.

These are business examples, but Phase B presents dangers in other situations too. Think about your job. Are you doing OK at the moment? You may well be but, if you take this for granted – assume that the success curve goes on forever – suddenly you find yourself being left behind by the hungrier, the better trained, the person with new ideas or the person not locked into the 'old way' of doing things. You tell yourself that your way is the right way because it has worked for you for so long, but you are fighting an unstoppable force. What worked for you for years may suddenly not work quite as well as it did.

Perhaps this even applies to leisure-time activities too. Taking up a hobby stimulates us because we are capturing our imagination and freshening ourselves up with an injection of new energy. One of the great things about taking up a hobby is that we find an almost never-ending avenue of possibilities within it. If we take up a new sport, we can constantly improve our skills. If we build model aeroplanes out of matchsticks, we get better and better at building them and can add more complex details to them. If we fail to find the pleasure of exploration and improvement within our hobby, then the hobby soon becomes the rut and we give up or get bored with it.

By the time we arrive at Phase C, things have reached a plateau, and the things described in the last two paragraphs start to become a reality. We fail to update our skills, or we fail to notice that things are changing because we are being successful – and before we realize it we are into Phase C and the stimulation curve is flattening. Of course when we reach Phase C some of us begin to realize that we have reached a plateau, so we begin to search for opportunity. We may find we need to make a discomfiting giant leap because things have moved on substantially – at least more so in Phase C than Phase B. Others don't do so until the curve is well and truly on the way down: Phase D.

So where do we grow our new opportunity curve? The answer is at the time we are most disinclined to – during Phase B. It may be that we do recognize that things are changing quickly and that we do need to make the big leap. Ryanair is again a good example here. Ryanair was bumbling along for many years as Ireland's second biggest carrier. It decided to change its modus operandi completely and become a 'no frills' carrier. At the same time, it changed its pricing model so that the earlier you booked the cheaper the flight (flights for 1 euro!).

Or it may be that we just feel that our life is heading for a bit of a rut if we look at the way it is spreading out ahead of us – perhaps where we are moving from Phase B to Phase C. The current exchange of people between France and the UK is a good example here. Many of the comfortably-off middle-aged English middle class are moving to France – they want a new stimulus in their lives. At the same time many young French are heading in the

Building a new opportunity curve

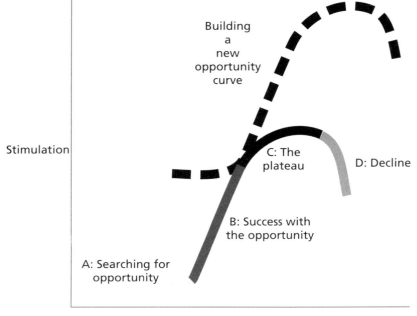

Building
a
new
opportunity
curve

Stimulation

C: The
plateau

D: Decline

B: Success with
the opportunity

A: Searching for
opportunity

Time

opposite direction, seeking opportunities in a more liberal and less restrictive economic climate. As former French Prime Minister Jean-Pierre Raffarin once said to British Prime Minister Tony Blair, 'You are giving us your middle-aged and we are giving you our young.'

You may find it a useful exercise to start thinking about your own opportunity curves. You may have many of them relating to career, family, leisure and so on. It may be that you feel that your life is in a rut and that a complete change is needed to fire up all the curves and grow new ones out of old. Are you in Phase C – at the pinnacle but perhaps subconsciously realizing that the good times may not last for ever? Or maybe on the upward curve in Phase B where things seem great but where it's important to start asking where you are going to next?

The lesson here is to try to build on the success of Phase B and open up a new avenue of opportunity, rather than wait for the slippage in Phases C and D where we have a more pressing problem to solve. This theme of opportunity spotting and problem solving will now be explored further.

We are afraid to approach the fathomless, bottomless groundlessness of everything.

R. D. Laing, *The Politics of Experience*

Stage 1(a)
Opportunity spotting – the search engine

❑ The search engine

❑ Who, why, what, where, when, how

❑ Feeling helpless

There is no single formula for opportunity spotting, in the same way that there is no unique formula for happiness. There are a series of ways of thinking about yourself, your life and the world you live in, that may make it easier for you to spot opportunities that are right for you. Because we are all so different and have so many experiences that have got us to the point we are at now, all that we need to propel us forward might be a suppleness of mind about ourselves and the possibilities that exist in our lives. In this section, where we concentrate on Stage 1(a) – opportunity spotting – the approach is to provide some ways of thinking that will help us to flex ourselves mentally so that we see more, and see it in a way that reflects the kinds of individuals we are. In Part Two, we work with 12 tools for opportunity takers – many of these will enhance the challenge of opportunity spotting.

Roger von Oech suggests the Explorer here (you may find it useful to refer back to the chart on page 26) because good opportunity spotters are the ones who go out and actively seek possibilities in the world around them. His Explorer metaphor is a useful tool in helping us to think about the challenge and the mentality required at this crucial stage.

■ The search engine

My previous book, *Positive Thinking, Positive Action*, introduced the idea of a 'search engine' mentality as a way of seeking out the possibilities and the opportunities that the world presents for us. In the same way that a search engine such as Google, Alta Vista or Yahoo opens up to us a seemingly never-ending world of information and possibility, the same applies to the psychology of the pure, uncluttered world of freeform opportunity spotting. When we search on the internet we suggest to the search engine a topic of interest – opportunity spotting, for example! – and at the click of a button we get connected to a mass of information and perspectives on the subject.

The randomness here can be enriching too. We often get responses to our request for information that appear almost totally unrelated to that which we were asking for. It can be mentally stimulating to take the mind off something we are searching hard for, but it can also identify a new avenue of opportunity for us. We may find our perspective being challenged so that we look at old problems in new ways. Or we identify an idea in our own imagination that can often take us off into random but rewarding paths frequently unconnected to the path we were travelling on before.

Random connection – something from nothing

Our brain has the remarkable capacity to make connections between things that 'out of nothing' create the seeds of invention. In the 24 hours before I was going to write this section of the book, I made a note of random ideas that came into my head and sought to expand them. The first of them is extremely bizarre, but the thought occurred to me as I was pondering it – I bet there's someone working on it right now. Here are the three thoughts I had:

1 Have you noticed how sports people no longer 'drink water'? Instead they 'rehydrate'. When I heard the word 'rehydration' spoken by an athlete, I immediately imagined them to be 'freeze dried', or a powder which with a little application of water could be bought back to life. Rather like the way we add water to rehydrate dried foods. Which got me thinking further. What about those ashes on the mantelpiece? Or wouldn't it be cheaper if we wanted to fly ourselves to the other side of the planet if we could freeze-dry the family and reconstitute them on arrival?

2 The retail phenomenon that is IKEA has a reputation for affordable, stylish home furnishings – many of them made from low-cost, wood-based products. A friend of mine who spends most of his working life moving IKEA furniture in his van said to me with typical black humour, 'They'll bury me in an IKEA coffin as well.' Which got me thinking. Has IKEA thought about a range of low-cost coffins? Or has anyone else thought of entering the low-cost coffin business?

3 As I proudly announced to my partner that I had written 1,000 words of this book in the previous two hours, her disbelieving comment was, 'Are you sure someone isn't writing it for you?' Which got me thinking again. What if we could write books through predictive text like we do when we write text messages on our mobile phones? Or why not cut 1,000 random words or sentences out of newspaper, put them in a bucket and draw them out when you need inspiration? It's said that we all have a book in us, so there must be a lot of first-novel writers looking to develop their plot but wondering how.

As two of these ideas relate to death, I started to wonder if my mood was a particularly dark one in the previous 24 hours – but I can say that I had a lot of fun with these ideas. And I really only scratched the surface in describing the directions in which my thoughts took me. So the key here is that we have opportunity spotting thoughts continuously, but perhaps don't even see them that way. Of course, if we acted on all of them we would never be able to commit enough time to any. But it does prove that our capacity to spot opportunities is inexhaustible – even when our brain is not in obvious 'opportunity spotting' mode. Being a little playful with your thoughts may be all that is required.

■ Who, why, what, where, when, how

> *I keep six honest serving men.*
> *They taught me all I know.*
> *Their names are What and Why*
> *and When, and How and Where*
> *and Who.*
> Rudyard Kipling

Think of all those times we've said, 'Wouldn't it be better if…?' Or 'What if…?' Or 'What this town really needs is…' Or 'Wouldn't it be great if we could go to…?' We display our capacity to spot opportunities all the time. The next step, if we want to act on the opportunity, or at least explore it a little further, is to say 'Why not?' Or better still, 'Why not me?'

What aren't you seeing?
Did you ever have an opportunity in your hand but didn't see it for what it was?

We are currently experiencing the dawn of nano-technologies which are going to change our lives for ever. One such nano invention actually occurred many years ago and was utilized by the Austrian skiing team. They applied microscopic glass balls to the bottom of their skis so that they would slide over the snow with almost no friction – the glass beads fill up all the tiny divots and ruts on the skis to create a perfectly smooth surface. This means that the skis go faster. Think about what that might mean in other environments. We know for example that a sheet of glass, placed under a microscope, has a surface akin to the moon's. Place these microscopic glass balls on to a glass surface and they effectively fill in the divots.

One application currently being marketed is as a surfactant for car windscreens. When muck hits the windscreen, it has nothing to adhere to because all the divots on the glass have been filled in. This means it slides off and you have a permanently clean windscreen. Other possibilities are being explored – think about the potential of these glass beads as a cleaning agent for glass.

This invention hung around for many years until a group of enterprising Germans saw the potential and commercialized the idea. Sometimes opportunities do exist in front of our eyes. What could you be missing because you are not choosing to 'see'? What knowledge do you have that could be applied in new circumstances?

And the competition is already kicking in! Another German scientist spent many years studying why it was that the leaves of the lotus plant, when immersed in water and then removed, would emerge with no water residue on them. Under a powerful microscope it was possible to see that, although to the naked eye the surface appears smooth, it is actually incredibly rough, with up to ten million 'rough edges' per pinhead. Nothing can cling to it! Glass has now been developed that has similar properties and we can see that very quickly the windows on your house would not need to be cleaned because no dirt would adhere to them.

Now that the idea of things never needing to be cleaned has created a new paradigm, we will see an explosion of nano-technologies destroying the old 'get on your hands and knees and clean it' pattern.

Both of these opportunities have come by applying knowledge from one situation to another completely different situation. Look outside your own small cosy world sometimes for your own opportunities. Who knows what might be found elsewhere?

What can I do?

We restrict our capacity to spot opportunities when we have a limited view of what we are capable of. If asked to make a list of five things of which we are capable, it is interesting how many people struggle to complete even this simple list. And yet we are all clearly capable of so much more than five things. A parent will identify a huge number of roles they have to perform when nurturing a child. A person who helps run a sports club can demonstrate strong organizational and interpersonal skills.

The next time you're sitting down with a friend, try this simple exercise. For five minutes have a conversation with them where you have to find out as much as you can about them *without* you telling them about yourself. The last time I did this, I discovered that the person I was talking to played for the Great Britain over-35 ice-hockey team and was an aficionado of what's known as Northern Soul music. I concentrated on ice-hockey and discovered a whole raft of things about this person – including his capabilities. If I subsequently asked him what he felt his capabilities were (and still are), I suspect his response may not have been as extensive as my list of his capabilities.

So when we spot opportunities, do we do so according to our own view of our own potential?

It is only when we test ourselves out that we begin to understand the capacity for the extraordinary that exists within us. When we hear remarkable stories of human endeavour, endurance and survival we begin to realize how far we can stretch ourselves.

You have to believe this. You can choose to get lost in the world of six billion or you can choose to be an active player within it. Every one of us has the capacity to be one of those players. Every one of us has a raft of capabilities with which to show the best side of ourselves to the world. One thing is certain. If we try to do little, we will never know how far we could have got. Try something – and who knows how far you can go? Who knows what roads will open up? The roads may lead to a far more interesting and stimulating life. And at least you will have learnt much more about yourself than you knew before.

What do I want in my life?

If we consciously make decisions to pursue particular opportunities in our lives, those decisions are likely to be based around the things we want, or believe we want, in life. If you are using this book as a tool to identify opportunities for yourself (rather than, say, a casual bedside read), then you may find it useful to try and think about what it is you really want out of life. Really think about this. It can be easy to say, 'My first priority is to have lots of money, my second priority is to have a big successful business and my third priority is to travel the world when I have attained the first two!' But are those things that you really want or what you think you ought to be wanting?

Some of the categories listed below may help you to think about your priorities in different aspects of your life.

- Material things (possessions, money)
- Spiritual matters
- Family
- Adventure
- Pleasure
- Work/daytime occupation
- Sport
- Mastery of a skill (for example, playing a musical instrument)
- Intellectual stimulation

Feel free to add other categories yourself. We can then prioritize within each of the categories according to what's more important to us. You could use a star system to help you do this – five stars for top priority down to one star for lowest priority. For example, a 20-year-old might say that family is a low priority (and give it one or two stars), and adventure – perhaps a desire to travel – has a high priority (and therefore give it five stars).

Remember to visit this list regularly, because over time our priorities change. There is, however, a danger with this exercise. If we see opportunities within our own perhaps limiting frame of reference, we may be blind to the opportunity that comes from left field. And we sometimes assume that certain things are important to us because they should be. I have assumed that travel and adventure are important to a 20-year-old because I am stereotyping the life I believe a 20-year-old may want to live – but getting on in a career may be the number one priority for many 20-year-olds.

I can recall a conversation with a woman who said that for 20 years she told herself that she didn't want children. When she became pregnant and had a daughter in her mid thirties, she realized that a baby was exactly what she wanted – even though she still retained other things that were important to her, including her career.

What do I want to say about myself – what's my epitaph?

The quote on page 8 says what I want to say about my life at the end of it. What do you want to say about yours? It's not something we say at the end of it, but more a feeling about what we want to do with our life now.

Who is saying what?

We are all information junkies living in the information junkie age. We have more information more easily available to us than any previous generation. Newspapers at under a euro or a pound or a dollar provide fantastic value for money. The internet can help us to know anything about anything (and some things we probably don't want to know!). Many countries around the world had two or three television stations 20 years ago and many now have 200–300. So it has become much easier to pick up on trends if you are seeking opportunities in business, or information on clubs and societies for your leisure time, or help for families with children if you are looking to reactivate some 'me' time – or even just randomly seeking information that can take you off in a new and unimagined direction. Even with all this information so readily to hand, we still need to seek it proactively. It's just much easier to find than it once was.

When we seek information it can be easy to look one-dimensionally. That is to say we look at the things we are already interested in. If we do this, we see only things that fit our existing frame of reference. Read about things you know little about. Find out who is saying what. Find out what people are doing that you hadn't even thought of. One of the biggest barriers to opportunity spotting is to assume that we know everything (the 'intelligent') when in reality we all know so little when it is placed against how much there is we could know. Try to read and observe in areas outside your own current sphere of interest – who knows where a newly found interest may take you? After all, you don't want to stand still for the rest of your life, do you? Do you?

Doing something

Sometimes we just need to try something to see where it takes us. In my book *Positive Thinking, Positive Action* I told in detail the story of Helene. Helene found herself listening to the radio one day when she heard a singer telling the listeners that she thought almost anyone could sing, and what stopped them was that they didn't believe they could. The very next day Helene was passing the newsagent's and saw an advertisement in the window offering singing lessons. Remembering what she heard on the radio, Helene contacted the singing teacher and started lessons. After a few lessons the singing teacher suggested to Helene that she could actually sing rather well and could she put her forward for auditions for choirs? Well, the choir she ended up in wasn't your average choir. It was the London Philharmonic Choir. Helene now tours the world with the choir. And what I didn't tell you was that Helene was 67 when she started the singing lessons.

What opportunities could open up for you if you just took that small step?

Feeling helpless

It's here. Now. It's right in front of you. It always was and it always will be. But you can't see it because you're not looking. And there may be very good reasons why you're not looking.

Psychologist Martin Seligman once came up with the phrase 'learned helplessness'. When events in our lives don't follow 'the plan', or they shock or surprise us, we learn that the experience can be psychologically painful. Eventually we become immune to the pain, we sit there and take it, without offering a proactive approach to overcoming it. We just let life happen to us. What then happens is that we react passively to difficulties when there may be a relatively simple route to escape. We aren't even looking to escape – we say, 'If I sit here it will go away,' or we might say, 'I've taken this much already, a bit more won't make any difference.' We become expert in spotting the bad things around us and do not even see that there are good things (including great opportunities) OR that sometimes the bad can be turned into good (the problem that becomes the opportunity).

So are some of us just born with a feeling of helplessness and some of us born with a positive disposition? Can we learn to help ourselves?

Positive psychology comes from a very hard sense of realism about life. I wonder if we went back 500 years whether people at that time would have had an understanding of the word 'depression'? Life was brutally tough from day one, there was unlikely to be any hiding from this and as a consequence we either got on with living (and these were wild times too!) or we didn't survive.

Nowadays we don't have these brutal realities in comfortable western cultures. But because of this, we don't experience some of the bad things early enough to accept them as a part of living and move on. If we know that there are some tougher aspects to living and that they will happen to us, then we are better placed to overcome them.

Great opportunity spotters and takers will tell us that things probably haven't been that easy for them too. We all to a greater or lesser extent ride the rollercoaster. But those leading fulfilled lives will tell you that they probably did at least one of the following to overcome the 'blows':

1 They know that there will be problems, a downside, but with that expectation they tell themselves things that will help them overcome those challenges. This realism is crucial, and the earlier we adopt it, the better.

2 Taking a more proactive approach to the world short-circuits the road to helplessness on which some of us end up travelling. This is not some kind of fanciful notion. It is based in the hard realism that if we want to engage fully with our life and the things that happen in it, then we can do it only by assuming full personal responsibility for our existence.

OR (and remember we have just looked at opportunity spotting), they will take you on to Stage 1(b).

We know about volcanoes…after the eruption.

Stage 1(b)
What is the problem? – incompatibility

❑ Paradigm paralysis

❑ What is the problem?

❑ Incompatibility

❑ Recession as opportunity

In reality we often find ourselves problem solving rather than opportunity spotting in 'virgin' territory. It's a bit like medicine in contemporary society – doctors spend their time curing patients rather than taking the opportunity to make sure illnesses don't happen in the first place. This is of course a cheaper and more beneficial option in the long term but requires more effort in the short term. Problem solving can mean fire fighting, but take a more coherent and positive approach to problem solving and we could be nurturing the opportunities of the future. Problem solving can lead to the change in life that we all secretly crave but sometimes strive for only when we are really pushed into it. For example, a few years ago a big bank did a study over a period of time comparing people who had been made redundant by a large company set against those who had been kept on. Three years down the line a far higher proportion of those made redundant said they were more successful and fulfilled than those who had stayed with the old company.

Organizations are very good at running courses on 'problem solving' and many readers have probably attended one of them. What they are less good at is running courses on opportunity spotting. Perhaps it is because we still find it difficult to work with change that we apply an 'if it ain't broke don't fix it' mentality to many aspects of our lives, and this applies to organizations of all kinds too. There may be times when this approach works. More likely the approach will get us into trouble when we discover an incompatibility between our actions and the actions that the circumstances really require.

This is of course a gross generalization, which I freely admit to. The dramatic levels of progress made by humankind in the last 250 years illustrate our capacity for opportunity spotting and invention. Nonetheless, even when we are flushed with our initial successes, we try to repeat the success using the formula that worked for us in the first place. The only trouble is that one day we find that the goal posts have shifted and the old way doesn't work any more.

■ Paradigm paralysis

In the early 1990s, futurologist Joel Barker wrote an excellent book, *Paradigms: The Business of Discovering the Future*. The book neatly depicts the dangers of taking the reactive problem solving mentality rather than the proactive opportunity spotting mentality. Paradigms can be described as a set of rules that help us understand all the things in our world. For example, at the time of writing, the accepted paradigm for the propulsion of the motor car is the petrol/gasoline-powered internal combustion engine. We work with paradigms even when we perform the most basic tasks – we even have set paradigms about the way we get to work. The longer we operate within existing paradigms, the more we can become prone to what Joel Barker calls 'paradigm paralysis'.

Paradigm paralysis takes over when we are so heavily invested in the old way that we are blind to the new. Barker quotes a much used but classic example to illustrate his point. The Swiss watch industry held about 90 per cent of the world's watch market in sales up to 1970. They themselves invented the quartz watch but displayed it at watch fairs as a kind of curio. Passing Japanese companies (Seiko, for example) saw the opportunity, started to produce their own quartz watch and within ten years the Swiss watch industry had collapsed. The remarkable thing about this story is that the Swiss themselves had invented what Joel Barker calls 'the new paradigm of time keeping'.

We can ask similar 'paradigm-shifting' questions about ourselves. Public sector workers throughout Europe will know that the old paradigm of working in the public sector was 'a job for life'. The public sector tended to attract those for whom a single 'job for life' was an attractive proposition. We all know that this notion is now dying in many western democracies – public sector workers in countries such as France and Germany will be learning this painful lesson over the next ten years or so for themselves. The self-employed know only too well that depending on one source of income is a risky business unless they seek to build what Charles Handy calls 'the portfolio career' or to update their skills continually. Someone will come along to do what you do better, cheaper or faster (or perhaps all three). How would you respond to that?

We know how common it has been for men in particular to die in the two years after retirement, and one reason is through lack of occupation. The skills that had got them through working life are now no longer needed

– the paradigm that made them feel valuable suddenly disappears. The signs are that people are recognizing the danger of this now, and it is important that both men and women make provision for keeping themselves enjoyably occupied in retirement.

In the new millennium the music singles chart became almost irrelevant. A listings vehicle designed to help young people know what was selling was almost totally shunned by them. The reason was that sales were being measured by what sold in the shops (the old paradigm), while many people were buying their music via internet downloads (the new paradigm). Even this paradigm is shifting quickly because it seems likely that bands, singers and musicians may sell downloads directly to the public and will have little interest in being listed in a chart. There is some evidence for this happening already – particularly those who don't feel the need to have a formal recording contract. How might this affect record companies? How would this affect their sales paradigm?

As Joel Barker himself has said, 'When everything changes we all go back to zero.' However harsh this sounds, it can be said to be true. The change may not be as dramatic as what happened to the Swiss watch industry, but nonetheless this going back to zero can fundamentally change our lives. We are often completely aware of new paradigms, but choose to switch into denial mode or hope that the new paradigm will go away.

Enter the new paradigm early, or at least on time, and you can produce a new opportunity curve in your life. And the true entrepreneurs and inventors among you may even invent the new paradigms yourself!

This paradigm paralysis can exist in our personal life and provides a major barrier to opportunity spotting. We can quickly become institutionalized by our circumstances, we get stuck in the rut and begin to see our way as the only way. It takes a big effort to snap out of it.

■ What is the problem?

Before we go forward with our problem and try to build an opportunity out of it, we need to define what the problem actually is. Try this:

Gary has a 24-track music studio which he built himself. It contains all the things you might expect. Mixing desks, instruments and computer equipment fill every available space. Gary himself is a successful music engineer and producer. Several of his own tracks have made the charts. In recent years Gary has offered his studio for rent to those who want to record their own music. If you want Gary's expertise in the studio, you can hire him as well as the studio space.

The studio has worked well for Gary over the years. The problem is that in recent years the demand for him and his studio has dropped quite significantly. The reasons for this are clear. What we used to need a recording studio to create can be done on a home computer with a few software additions. Where we needed a technologically advanced engineer to create the right soundscapes in the past, the modern boy or girl in their bedroom has an in-built understanding of the technology because they have been bought up in that world.

So what should Gary do? He clearly has a problem. But what is the problem? Ponder this for a few seconds yourself before reading on.

The problem could be:

1 Gary's skills are now no longer needed.
2 Gary has a studio full of recording equipment which is not being used.
3 Gary has a space of about 25 square metres which is under-utilized.
4 Gary needs to obtain another source of income to survive.

There could be many others. How we define the problem will be critical as we move into the next phase where we download possible solutions to the problem. Clearly, if Gary himself defined the problem as Number 2, he might say, 'Let's sell all the equipment.' If he thought the problem was Number 1, he might say, 'The space isn't the problem at all, it's what to do with my skills.' This would mean that he would respond in a different way – possibly getting up to speed himself in the newest technologies (which in reality he has done).

What we see as the problem (or indeed if we change our thinking, the opportunity) will fundamentally affect how we respond to the problem Goal in the next stage – Stage 2.

Another example. Say you have a significant amount of debt through credit cards and loans. You could define your problem in a number of ways, which in turn suggest possible responses.

1 I am not earning enough money.
   Possible responses include:
   ■ Overtime
   ■ Second job
   ■ Get another, better-paid job
   ■ Rob a bank!
   ■ Take up gambling

2 I am spending too much money.
   Possible responses include:
   ■ Cut back on spending
   ■ Sell the house and buy a smaller, cheaper one/rent a cheaper house
   ■ Hand back credit and store cards

3 I am not managing my finances properly.
   Possible responses include:
   ■ Renegotiate terms with my debtors
   ■ Employ an accountant
   ■ Budget properly

We can see here how a redefinition of the problem immediately changes the range of responses. There will of course be considerable overlap – or we might decide that we have all these problems anyway. Nonetheless, as we move into the next 'What solutions are open to me?' stage – which we have touched on here – the parameters of possible responses change considerably depending on what we define as the original problem.

■ Incompatibility

Where a current problem creates the need to look for a new opportunity, we are recognizing an incompatibility between our current circumstances and the requirements of the future. Or worse, we realize that the world has overtaken us before we were even aware of it. At times like these, current methods may have ceased to be compatible with new realities. It might be that the skills you learnt during further education or in employment are no longer the right ones for your job, or that better-qualified people are available to do it. If you are in business, it might be that someone has come along with a better service or product or is challenging the very essence of your business.

When we looked at our opportunity curve earlier, we saw the dangers in taking our current circumstances for granted. It is always better to pre-empt the potentially difficult situation than have to respond to it when it's suddenly upon us. But that is no help if you are in this situation.

What can be helpful is to refer back to the previous section on opportunity spotting. We can decide to try to get ourselves back up to pace, much the same as the UK retail giant Marks and Spencer decided to do early this century. Another example came in the early 1990s when huge advances in computer technology were a potential threat to those who had been brought up with other means of communication. Some of the associated language appeared to be designed to turn off anyone over the age of 25! The reaction of many retirees was fascinating. Some switched off and decided it wasn't for them. Others decided that they wanted to be a part of what I consider to be one of the most exciting inventions of my lifetime (the internet), and now, some of the keenest internet users are retirees.

Recession as opportunity

For the reader in business, much inspiration can be found in the work of Tom Peters in the early 1990s. We've got a problem – impending recession or a downswing in our segment of the economy. What do we do? Do we do what everyone else does – slash the marketing, R&D and training budgets? Or do we do what our competitors aren't? The logic is simple. When the recession is over, do we want to be entering the upswing with untrained staff and with moderate customer awareness, when among the competition will be someone who took the opposite view? The way we see a problem will affect the way we respond. The way out of tough market conditions often comes when someone within your sector finds a way through the trouble. This might be through great marketing campaigns, great service (through your people), or great new products. It is unlikely to come through cutting everything.

Recession is a problem but it is also an opportunity. We can grab market share and leave ourselves accelerating out of the blocks when trading conditions improve. Some say the real opportunities for business lie in recession rather than economic upswings – it's where things get more interesting. It's where the potential to innovate really matters – how many organizations up the R&D budget at the time they most need to?

We need imaginative people in tough times. It's an easy option to slash budgets – and people – to the nth degree, but this will leave the core of what makes any business strong decimated when things improve.

So, if you are running your own business, a franchise or you are part of a management team as an employee, start to see the value of recognizing tough trading conditions as an opportunity. Almost all of your competitors will be in the same boat. What are you going to do that is different from them? It will change the way you look at Stage 2 – the download.

Just remember, if we are locked into a problem:

In the middle of every difficulty lies opportunity.
Albert Einstein

Whether we have spotted an opportunity – Stage 1(a) – or identified a problem – Stage 1(b) – we will have defined ourselves a simple goal. The goal will be something along the lines of: 'How can I make the most of this opportunity?' or 'How can I solve this problem?' Either way, we then move into Stage 2 of the process.

Let a riot in your thinking create a revolution in your life.

Stage 2
Possible solutions – the download

❏ The chat room

❏ Cut and paste

❏ It's hot in here and I need an ice-cream!

So we have our Goal. The Goal has been defined by a problem we are trying to solve or by an opportunity we have seen or created ourselves. In this next stage we now need to experiment and generate some possible answers that will help us bring the opportunity or the challenge created by the problem out into the open.

The phrase 'blue-sky thinking' has entered the lexicon of 'business-speak' to the point where the words themselves often elicit a collective groan from the cynical. Nonetheless the limitless, free nature of a pure blue sky neatly describes the mode of thinking in this stage. Roger von Oech uses the Artist as his role here because we associate art with creativity. We need to stretch our thinking so that we come up with solutions that are truly creative as well as solutions that come from more conventional approaches.

The object of the exercise is to generate as many possible answers to the problem or opportunity as possible. In other words to 'download' all the different ways we could approach the opportunity or problem Goal. It is interesting that the thinking behind this 'mental download' phase also has many applications in the initial 'search engine' phase. In the guidance at that stage we referred to questions like 'What if…?', 'Why don't we do it that way?', 'What might happen if…?' These are lines of questioning that work equally well in this stage too. Just remember that the golden rule is that all ideas are live ones. We should not be judgemental. We just need to get all our thoughts, ideas and inspirations out in the air and breathing. We do truly need to download. We are not in a position to judge the quality yet and neither should we be. Our concern is for quantity.

■ The chat room

This is not a call to try to generate ideas through an internet chat room – but it could be one method of addressing the need to find ideas through conversation and social interaction. Many of us will have heard the clichéd suggestion, 'Let's spark some ideas off each other.' But in effect that is what we are doing here. In a chat room there is a continual to-ing and fro-ing of comments, suggestions and ideas. A free-flowing and uninhibited expression of the conventional, the slightly out of the norm and the wild and wacky. And as in a chat room, we are continually building on the suggestions and ideas of other people. Unlike the chat room, however, we seek not to be critical but rather to embrace all shades of opinion and observation no matter how far beyond our own frame of reference they may be.

The key here is to suspend the temptation to compete by saying, 'That's rubbish because…' or 'We couldn't possibly do that because…' We save this for the next stage. Being judgemental at this stage will cause us to short-circuit what was a good healthy flow of ideas and suggestions.

▓ Cut and paste

In 'cut and paste' thinking we take our knowledge from one situation and apply it to another perhaps entirely different situation. Here is a challenge that illustrates perfectly what we mean by this.

Imagine you are in Africa and you have both a problem and an opportunity. The opportunity is that you have a plentiful supply of fresh water underground in an area that suffers continual water shortages. The problem is that there appears to be no source of energy to pump it out of the ground.

How might you respond? You may wish to try to do a mental download here and think of as many possible solutions to the problem as you can. Try it with a friend (the creative chat room!). Remember, this is not the stage where we apply critical thinking to the problem. So the solutions may vary from building a pipeline to shipping in a power supply to building a well and sending someone down with a bucket.

The actual solution was a classic example of 'cut and paste' creative thinking. Think about the word 'energy' and think about all the different sources of energy. Not just the obvious ones like gas and electricity. How about children?

There just so happened to be a roundabout in the village that the children loved to play with. By harnessing the energy generated from the roundabout when it was in use, the villagers were able to pump the water up to the surface. And there was always a ready supply of children ready to volunteer for roundabout duty!

■ It's hot in here and I need an ice-cream!

In the hothouse that is the generation of ideas, we need to keep cool. A clear separation of modes of thinking will help us. So here are three modes of thinking based around ice-cream flavours:

■ Vanilla

Where the solutions are the more obvious, simple ones.

■ Chocolate

Where connections are made between similar, but not the same, things – where a little bit of flavour has to be added to take our thinking beyond the norm. An example here might be the way that the bicycle evolved into the motorcycle.

In a more practical application, we know how to use a PC and apply our knowledge to using an AppleMac.

■ Neapolitan

Where we go freeform with our thinking and combine a series of unconnected thoughts, ideas and concepts. The child's roundabout story is a good one here because it links two previously unrelated things – roundabouts and water pumps. This Neapolitan thinking takes what we might call a multi-flavoured approach to the problem or the opportunity.

The sandwich bar

So let's apply our ice-cream thinking to another situation: the opportunity to open a sandwich bar in our local town. We are at the stage where we are deciding what types of sandwich fillings to offer our customers.

■ Vanilla

If there are no other competitors in the town, we might decide that just having a sandwich bar is an opportunity in itself and we may find it necessary to offer only conventional fillings – cheese, tuna, chicken, beef, salad and so on.

■ Chocolate

We still need bread and sandwich fillings but the offering may be a little more unconventional – English breakfast (sausage, bacon and egg), Sunday lunch (turkey, stuffing and a bit of veg) or Brie and grape are good examples here. These all exist but are much less common.

Why not offer one half of a sandwich instead of two (for which we might decide to charge two-thirds of the price of the 'whole' one)? I believe the sandwich chain Prêt à Manger now does this.

■ Neapolitan

What about sandwiches filled with ice-cream (linking two previously unconnected foodstuffs)? Children would love them.

What about bread-free sandwiches? I just want the tuna, not the bread!

What about 'air sandwiches' – well, some of us just like bread and butter!

What about naming the sandwiches after celebrities? Isn't that where the word sandwich came from anyway (the Earl of Sandwich)?

And while we're at it, we could be creative about whom we sell our sandwiches to. A true Neapolitan solution would be to come up with a special sandwich for pet owners. How about Pedigree Chum sandwiches! It's rare that we see sandwiches that might appeal more to the palate of children – are there opportunities here?

I want more ice-cream!

Just remember: with Neapolitan thinking we may come up with solutions that seem totally mad. But yesterday's madness is today's normality – amid the madness could be the golden nugget. If we just wanted to keep with the ice-cream theme, think about the way Ben and Jerry's named their ice-cream flavours – one of them 'Cherry Garcia' after Jerry Garcia, singer/guitarist with rock group The Grateful Dead. It's my favourite ice-cream – but if someone had suggested it to me ten years ago I might have laughed at them.

How about this for the future? What about naming the flavour of an ice-cream after the breed of cow that produced the cream for the ice-cream you're now eating? The best cream produces the best ice-cream and the different breeds of cow produce different qualities of milk for the ice-cream. We do it with wine now. Why not ice-cream?

Whoever imagined we'd be eating 'hedgehog' crisps? And they don't have any hedgehog in them. We should complain!

Paranoia means having all the facts.

William Burroughs

Stage 3
Making right decisions – filtering

❏ Filtering

❏ Dave's story

❏ The waiting game

In this stage Roger von Oech describes us as thinking like a Judge. Here we sift the evidence, get some expert opinions and advice and try to make what we believe will be the right decision based on the information we have. After the freewheeling mental approach of the previous stage we now have to put the brakes on and decide what ideas and actions will help us to make the most of the opportunity we have now identified. In effect, what we are doing in this stage is putting all the information we have through a giant mental filter which will help us decide the best course of action. This is why I call this the 'filtering' stage.

This stage requires the best of two critical factors:

1   Quality and relevance of information.

2   A large healthy dose of intuition.

The key question to start with is, how much information do you need? Human beings are very good at picking up a whole load of mental spam which immediately gets mixed up with all the quality information. As a result, what's important to us gets diluted with irrelevancies. This could potentially include the opinions and perspectives of almost anyone we may care to ask for advice. Some of this advice will be valuable, some will be highly prejudiced by the world-view of that person – but it may be hard to know which is which.

We can make a case for doing almost anything. These days so much information is available to us (to which I confess this book is adding!) that almost anything is believable and therefore possible. This is a good thing. It can be helpful to know that others have experienced similar problems and can pinpoint a way forward. Do remember, however, that no two situations are alike.

The difficulties come when we operate in environments where the rule-book has yet to be written. A genuinely innovative idea will have little or no precedent that could help us make the right decision concerning it. In this situation we will have to rely on intuition or 'gut feeling' and bravery to find a way forward. There are some wonderful examples here. Consider the boldness (and sometimes bravery) involved in some of the following:

- Discovering a new world – explorers of five to six centuries ago through to modern-day astronauts
- Mary Wollstonecraft, 'the first feminist', writing in the late 18th century – so far out of kilter with contemporary thought that some of her ideas would seem radical even now
- Stravinsky's *Rite of Spring*
- Giving your bone marrow

■ Filtering

When we make decisions we put together all the information we have, from whatever source, and try to make sure that what comes out contains no impurities that may damage the decision-making process. Decision making requires clear, pure thinking. Good decision making requires us to test our decisions against our own:

- Opinions and prejudices
- Psychological spam
- Available time

Opinions and prejudices

Are you letting your bias and personal preferences cloud your judgement? What assumptions are you making that it might be helpful to challenge?

Just because you like certain things, what evidence do you have that others share your interests and desires?

Are you listening too much to the opinions of others whose views may be as one-sided as your own?

Filter your decisions through the lives and thinking of others and challenge yourself to see the world in other ways. Rational, cool thinking, with a good dose of added intuition, will filter out the impurities.

BUT

Balance this with the uniqueness of your world-view. You might be seeing the great business opportunity, the chance for adventure or the retirement interest that will take your life to another level – if that is what you seek. Value your unique perspective but don't be a slave to it.

Psychological spam

We rarely make decisions about opportunities with absolutely no supporting evidence. The evidence may not extend much further than our intuition, but we will usually have something other than just gut feeling to hang on to. Nonetheless many of us run the risk of making no decision at all because we require an overload of information to justify the decision we are about to take. It is the poison of the large corporation when the paranoid manager says, 'Write me a report on it,' when you confront him or her with your new idea. What they are doing is asking you to prepare their excuses for them in case of failure.

If we rely on complete information to make the best decision, we may never have enough. We end up grinding to a halt with information overload because we can no longer see what is relevant and what isn't.

Don't strangle the opportunity under the weight of meaningless information and data.

BUT

Don't rely on pure intuition to guide you in the right direction. Our intuition is not infallible. We can convince ourselves that something is right even when it isn't, through falling in love with our ideas and beliefs.

Available time

So how long do we spend making decisions? If I wait too long, will the opportunity have gone? If I jump in too quickly, will I be ignoring some issues? These issues apply to seekers of business opportunities. What is clear is that we can get side-tracked by irrelevancies if we are falling prey to information overload.

The rule here is that there are no rules. Many opportunities exist for our whole lives. Sometimes we spend ages getting round to taking an opportunity, taking up a new hobby or changing jobs for example, and then wonder why we didn't go for it years ago. Sometimes the decision needs to take about as long as it took to think up the idea. About five seconds!

You have a virus!

What's tough about making decisions is that we can find our emotions heightened to the point that our thinking may not be as clear as it should be. The purity of thought required at this stage is difficult to find because there might be certain factors that are influencing this course of action.

If you are responding to a problem in Stage 1(b) it may be that the problem has angered you. Perhaps you were made redundant, or you didn't get the promotion you deserved, or you have very noisy neighbours. Action is required but anger can be a very damaging emotion. It can cause us to take actions that we might regret. Negative thoughts can hijack reason and we send ourselves down what could be a vengeful and counter-productive path.

If we consider some of the great figures of the 20th century, we might come up with such names as Nelson Mandela, Gandhi and Ang Sang Suu Kyi. All three have or had every justification for anger, having spent significant parts of their lives in jail. And yet all three showed no malice. It is certain that the flame of anger never stopped burning, but their energies were channelled into changing society through peaceful means.

Dave's story

I worked for a single company for most of the 1990s. I was very successful and I like to think I earned the respect of our customers and suppliers for my professional attitude. We were the second biggest company in the market-place, and what drove us was the desire to keep snapping at the heels of the company who were top. Although the industry sector we worked in could be described as a cottage one, we felt important. Well, important enough that we were motivated to keep inspired about what we were doing! We were an innovative organization because we had to be. We didn't have the profile of the top brand and what happened is I suppose typical of what happens when the biggest brand gets a bit bored of fighting off the number two. They bought us!

Many friends were made redundant. I got taken on into the newly merged business and I hated it. That's not quite right to say I hated it.

I convinced myself I would hate it before I even went there and I never gave it a chance. My emotions and energies were channelled towards destruction. Eventually I left and the very day I left I was offered a product to distribute by a supplier to the top brand. They were backing me rather than my previous employer.

Such was my inbuilt anger at what had happened that I thought this was my chance to get my own back. I was stupid – I took a great opportunity and used it for entirely negative ends. I set out to be destructive – my marketing was geared towards knocking my previous employer (legal but pointless) and contacting previous customers of my old employer (legally unclear but thoughtless). The details are less important here and the actions shrouded in grey areas but ultimately my former employer took me to court and I settled before the case went to the High Court. I learned the danger of channelling my justified anger into a totally damaging and pointless action. I now think about all my actions first and make sure that I make decisions to do things with the best of motives. The sad part was that the opportunity was a great one. My actions in making it happen were not so great! I've moved on but remembered.

■ The waiting game

Imagine you're a card player. You're playing a poker game and the stakes are high. You think you hold a winning hand (the great opportunity) but you are considering some of the options open to you. Think about what those options might be:

■ You could play your hand now, and not benefit from the gains you would have made had you held your potentially winning hand for longer.

■ You could save yourself from a big defeat later on for a smaller gain now. Less risk but you miss out on the big win.

■ You could opt for a less rational decision-making process that relies on your instinct to show your hand at exactly the right moment.

What would you use to try and make the best decision?

- **Experience** What worked in previous situations like this? Or is this the first time you've ever played the game? Remember, though, that no two situations are alike.

- **Probability** What is the likelihood that other people hold better hands? Again, your previous experiences may play a part.

- **Intuition** A 'feeling' that what you have is better than anyone else's hand. Can you get a 'feel' from the clues that others are sending out?

- **Head and heart** Things are going OK but don't let the excitement of the moment mean that your emotions run away from your rational, more measured side. The best decisions need a combination of the two – what I call 'Whole…Heart…Head' decisions. Can you control your emotions to the extent that you don't reveal your pleasure at what you think is a winning hand? Can you control your emotions enough that you don't make a bad decision? Controlling heightened emotion may lead to better decisions and greater rewards.

- **Opportunity** If I don't take the opportunity now, would I ever? This is a great chance for me. I must not let myself become so obsessed by doing the right thing that I become paralysed into doing nothing.

Key points
Applying experience, probability, intuition, the 'head' and the 'heart' and a sense that 'this is the time' can all help us make better decisions. But the natural resource that is our intuition will often be sharpened by life's experiences.

You are right and I am wrong!
Why not play devil's advocate by arguing against your own preferences? It will help you thrash out the key issues and the salient points. This is a real discipline that will help retain a vital sense of balance in your own thinking and help prevent you seeing your future through a one-dimensional set of arguments. We all have multi-dimensional minds but sometimes need to work harder to find those dimensions, those other ways of seeing the world.

The pink one or the green one?

It may seem strange, but a more flexible mind may actually make this decision-making phase tougher. The flexible mind will create more possible solutions in the download phase, with the result that in this more judgemental phase we have to whittle down the number of possible solutions.

Here is one possible route. Those of you who have children will know that if you say to a child, 'What top do you want to wear today?' you may end up waiting half an hour for an answer! 'This one...no *this* one... can I try this one?' Sharp parents know that by saying, 'Which top do you want to wear, the pink one or the green one?' your child is more likely to come up with an instant answer.

If you don't know what course of action to take, just be brutal and cross some of the options out. Get it down to a choice of two and see if it is any easier to come to a decision.

The point here is that if you are struggling to come up with what you want to feel is the right solution, then you may need to be brutal with some of the possible solutions. It is often said that the key is less about agonizing over the rightness or wrongness of a decision and more about actually making any decision and making it work for you.

Did you ever exchange a glance with someone on the down escalator when you are on the up? And then think, 'If only...'?

Stage 4
Going live – you are connected!

❏ Renewal

❏ Realism

❏ Reward

❏ Responsibility

Here we reach that time when our decision breathes fresh air and is exposed to the rigours of survival in the outside world. This stage is all about acting on the opportunity. Roger von Oech refers to this as the Warrior stage. As he himself says, 'If you want your idea to succeed, you'll have to take the offensive. So you become a warrior and take your idea into battle… you develop your strategy and commit yourself to reaching your objective… you may have to overcome excuses, idea-killers, temporary setbacks and obstacles.'

This stage requires the impact of your positive mental attitude to overcome the troughs and make the most of the peaks as you seek to develop your opportunity. The struggle within your own mind to create opportunities and ideas gets transferred to the wider world, and the warrior mentality needs to take over to make the most of the opportunity you see. Taking the opportunity – giving it the green light – in your mind requires a mindset based in hard work and the willingness to tough it out when required.

The opportunity we have identified is now living and breathing in the real world with all the ups and downs that life presents for us. We have made the connection between the opportunity as an idea or a possibility, and it can be helpful now to adopt the '4 Rs' of true connection with our internal and external world:

- Renewal
- Realism
- Reward
- Responsibility

■ Renewal

Try to answer the following three questions:

1 When did you last have a feeling of being truly 'alive'?
2 When was the last time that you tried something for the first time?
3 What was the last thing that you can remember 'learning'?

If you can pinpoint answers to these questions without thinking very hard and can place your answers in the very recent past, then you probably are one of those who seek to inject stimuli into life so that you do have that feeling of being truly 'alive'. The reality for most of us is that the answers to these questions will come, but it will be a struggle to find them. The answers will be firmly locked in the past and we may be struggling to find the keys that unlock that particular memory.

In fact, our desire at the very least to 'freshen up', and at the other extreme to renew ourselves and our lives, drives all the four stages highlighted in this part of the book. The more we desire some kind of renewal, the more we are likely to seek opportunities in the first place. However, renewal is placed solidly in the fourth phase because, as Roger von Oech suggests in what he calls the Warrior stage, overcoming setbacks and obstacles will be an intrinsic part of our experience in this stage. What will be tested here will be your desire to really go for it – how much do you really want that renewal? Pretending to yourself that you do will mean getting caught out early in this stage. The business start-up that encounters a few problems in the early days (as they surely will) will soon back out. The person who joins an exercise club and only goes twice because it's too much like hard work. The person who goes to language class and then backs out because the romance of the opportunity didn't connect with the reality.

If you didn't do it, it was because you didn't want to do it enough. That may sound harsh, but in most situations it will be true.

When did you last have a feeling of truly being 'alive'?

- Athletes love the 'natural high' they get after exercise.
- People who enjoy their job love the feeling of making a contribution.
- Entrepreneurs love the feeling that they are their own boss.

In this stage we truly express ourselves and our individuality to the world. If your opportunity in action gives you these feelings of being alive, then go for it. It doesn't mean that there won't be pain and disappointment. What it does mean is that the pain and disappointment will be worth it.

When was the last time that you tried something for the first time?
The list of first-time experiences could go on forever but might include:

- Starting a business
- Parachuting
- A weekend away somewhere you have never been before
- Applying for a job in a new environment or industry
- Taking up a language
- Buying a franchise
- Eating a new kind of foreign food
- Sexual experimentation
- Listening to a new kind of music/learning a new instrument
- Joining a third-agers' adventure club

What was the last thing that you can remember 'learning'?

Learning gets to the heart of what personal renewal really means. It is too easy to suggest that we do all our learning in childhood. Certainly those who believe this to be the case won't recognize the opportunity to improve and learn from experience in adulthood. Learning requires a little humility. It's OK to say, 'I don't know.' It's even better to say, 'I don't know but I'm going to find out.'

Of course we all have opportunities to learn throughout our lives, but we can be prone to learning stagnation if we aren't prepared to acknowledge that we learn right up to the end.

■ Realism

What do we do when times get a bit tough? Which they will. We're out there on the open road, making the most of our opportunities, when something comes along to test us – perhaps this is why Roger von Oech describes us as needing Warrior-like tendencies (see page 72) – and life becomes a bit tougher than before. Our own personal sense of realism can help us recognize that, no matter how committed we are to the opportunity, there will be a dark side that will challenge all of our psychological resources. This darker side, perhaps the events that we cannot predict, will provide searching questions about our determination to succeed.

Creating a protective shell

If we take a realistic stance early enough in the stages (particularly in the third decision-making stage), we will have already recognized that there will be tough times, even if we can't be certain what form these tough times will take. It's at this time that we need to build an insulating shell around us to propel ourselves forward into the future. This may be a series of self-affirming statements that get us through the 'slap in the face' moment.

Early realism helps us to say, 'I know this feeling, I knew it could happen but I say "…" to myself to get me through it.'

A good example may be the marathon runner who has trained for six months for their first marathon. When they hit the famous 'wall' at the 20-mile mark, a whole host of feelings will work through their head, the most powerful of which will be 'I want to stop'. But the feeling that builds up in us as we contemplate non-completion is the letting down of friends, those charities for which we may be running, and of course ourselves. But what pushes us on is the 'I am going to finish this race' statement that provides the insulating shell against the circumstances we will surely encounter.

These shell statements, if we say them to ourselves, regularly help build confidence in our ability to knock down the barriers we will confront.

So as you consider what the tough times may feel like, build up two or three shell statements that will move you forward.

Hard work

In Stage 4 we need to recognize that opportunity taking can be tough. Those who start a new business need to know that they are committing themselves to 10–12 years – and possibly a lifetime – of incredibly hard work. If you are not prepared to commit to that, then you may as well forget the idea and pass on the opportunity to somebody who is prepared to make that commitment.

I recall an estate agency starting up in my part of South London a few years ago at the height of the property boom. A perfect time, you might think, to take the opportunity to get a property business started. Rising prices and a ready market of buyers and sellers made for a vibrant market. How could they fail?

They failed because they weren't open very often. For any business it's a good idea to be open when your customers are around. For an estate agent this means Saturday, Sunday and lunchtimes. This may be inconvenient to the estate agent but highly convenient for customers. My local start-up estate agent managed Saturday morning but Sunday and lunchtimes were usually out of the question. Hard-working competitors would be open on a Sunday – because the customers were around with a bit of time on their hands. My estate agent didn't last long. The simple truth is that starting a new business is very, very hard work.

And always ask what you could be doing that your competitors aren't doing. What can you add that will send that bit of business your way rather than in another direction?

> *Because I know my competitors aren't.*
>
> Daley Thompson, the great Olympic decathlete, on being asked why he trained on Christmas morning

◼ Reward

So with all this hard work, all this realism, all the disappointments, why bother taking up new opportunities? This is perhaps the toughest question to answer. To put in the effort required in any of the stages, but particularly so in Stage 4 (because the effort required may last a lifetime), we have to believe that the extra effort is worth it. We are likely to deliver our best only when we have convinced ourselves that the rewards merit the effort we put in. What we define as a reward is, however, the toughest question to answer!

How 'rich' do you want to be?

> *America is, as I am constantly reminded, a rich country. But not a country where everyone can be rich.*
>
> Writer and broadcaster Charles Handy, *Beyond Certainty*

It depends, I suggest, how you define 'rich'. Readers from Australia, South Africa, Europe or the UK all live in countries with great possibilities for personal monetary wealth. With the non-financial wealth of possibility and opportunity in all of these countries, the potential for a life of enrichment is massive.

For some readers the rewards will be highly tangible – and money is a prime motivator for at least some of us. For others the rewards may be less explicit but just as motivating. For the retiree, having the time and the desire to explore the world, the rewards may come as mental stimulation. For the competitors among us, it may be a desire to pit your capabilities against the world and see if you come out on top. For the business start-up, it may be the feeling that you have control over your working life – you are empowered. For someone working for a charity, the rewards may be the satisfaction of altruism.

These all present very good reasons to take on opportunities because the rewards are reflected in what we seek out of life. And we all seek different things. To borrow a contemporary cliché, what floats my boat may well not float yours. Listen to yourself and what you really want out of life.

The dangling of a reward carrot is what helps to keep us going in tough circumstances. When the reward ceases to mean anything or if we can't put in the effort required to achieve the rewards we seek, then it may well be time to stop and go and do something else.

■ Responsibility

So your opportunity is now a reality. With that reality comes a healthy dose of personal responsibility. In an age where we are encouraged to believe that everything that happens to us is somebody's else's fault it can be a challenge in itself to reflect back on ourselves and ask, 'What can I do that will make a difference?' Here are some suggestions that will help us to take personal responsibility at all stages of the OST process, but particularly in the stage where we are 'alive' and in the real world.

1 Confront difficulties and challenges. Don't ignore them

No one is going to solve your difficulties for you – apart from you. The longer we leave problems, the bigger they get. So, regardless of our circumstances, we can always be proactive in dealing with current challenges.

2 Take personal responsibility for your successes and failures

If something isn't quite working for you in your new opportunity, ask what you can do to make the difference next time. We cannot worry about external factors over which we have little personal control. As one might say, 'Stuff happens.' But we can control our personal reaction and use it as a learning experience so that we stand a better chance of getting it right when we hit difficulties in the future.

3 Be positive

A relentless analysis of what's going wrong can make us feel like we are failing. And what's more, we can lose our confidence if the setbacks are all we see. Remember, there are always things that are working and it's important to keep them in mind. Don't psychologically beat yourself up over the 20 per cent that needs improving. Remember the 80 per cent that is working!

4 You've got to enjoy it!

When we take opportunities, we are doing so because we feel they will enhance and enrich our life and possibly the lives of others. The enjoyment may be greater in hindsight but nonetheless the enjoyment of taking opportunities and consequently feeling as though we are taking control of our life cannot be replaced. Don't forget to enjoy it.

5 How good am I?

OK, you're doing well. But don't take your strengths for granted. Professionals work on strengths as well as weaknesses. In the 1990 World Cup the English football team lost to Germany on a penalty shoot-out. It transpired that Germany had practised their penalties in training and England hadn't. Who were the professionals?

6 Visualize success

There is nothing as motivating as believing that we can be an achiever. If we give ourselves a sense of what success feels like, we provide ourselves with a sensory driver that will push us towards the rewards we seek. If we can't see success, or don't believe that we can succeed, we may struggle to make the most of the opportunity.

7 You are free to choose an attitude

Remember, the indivisible freedom we have is to choose the attitude we bring to a situation no matter what the situation.

8 It's never too late to start...

No matter what your age, circumstances, financial status or previous calling, you can wake up to life full of possibility if you want to. This is not a glib statement. There are people in worse circumstances than you taking up even the slightest possibility of an opportunity, while others bemoan their current situation.

The end

And so we reach the end of the final stage. Or perhaps we don't! The 4 Rs of opportunity taking in Stage 4 sit very comfortably with the crystal clear thinking required in Stage 1(a) – opportunity spotting. The best opportunity takers, if they are to continue to do this, will find themselves living not in the linear process defined on page 25, but in the cyclical process we see below – and where many of the core skills overlap. We don't spot and take opportunities once in our life. We find we can do it all the time!

The 4-stage cycle

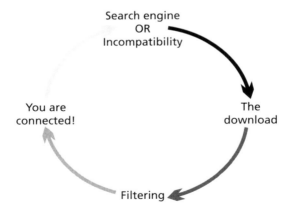

*When you find the opportunity
you seek,
Or if the opportunity finds you,
Nurture it.
And secure your grip.*

Part Two
The opportunity taker's tool-kit

- ❏ 1 The wall
- ❏ 2 Terra incognita – unknown land
- ❏ 3 Change your conditioner
- ❏ 4 Great success from minor disaster!
- ❏ 5 The third age
- ❏ 6 Open for business
- ❏ 7 Fruit picking
- ❏ 8 One thing leads to another…
- ❏ 9 Capturing the imagination
- ❏ 10 Future thinking
- ❏ 11 Building relationships
- ❏ 12 Getting motivated

We now have our structure for successfully spotting and taking opportunities. This structure will serve you well. Even with opportunities that we have to take quickly, there is no reason why this process cannot be worked through equally speedily. Where time is available – and indeed some opportunities are open to us for our whole lives – the structure will become even more appropriate. Don't, however, use it in a way that paralyses you. The structure should always be a catalyst, a spur to taking successfully the opportunities you (or others) have identified.

So how can we apply the structure? Models are always simplifications of reality, so we now need to create some sense of what it feels like to apply some of this thinking to our lives. This part of the book brings the theory and the actuality together. It's divided into 12 distinct sections that are designed to do two things:

1 Give some guidance on how to spot and take opportunities in particular situations for example, starting a business or retirement.

2 Suggest some positive approaches that will help maximize the potential we have to make the most of our opportunities for instance, 'the wrecking ball' and 'conditioning'.

We all live in unique circumstances. No two lives are the same. But as we assess people's lives we can begin to pick up patterns of behaviour that suggest that successful opportunity takers do share some characteristics – even if their temperaments and personalities will be diverse. So, as we look at different situations where being a successful OST will reap dividends, we will also assess the lives of a wonderful group of positive people. Only one or two are well known. The majority are living lives away from the media. I believe we are all capable of extraordinary things as our opportunity takers in this book will attest. It is such a sadness that so few of us get anywhere near fulfilling our capabilities. Perhaps the reasons are that we maybe don't believe we can, or we don't know how to. There is no set formula that guarantees success, but nonetheless we can learn from people who have successfully spotted and taken their opportunities.

For the rest of us, remember: all it takes is one small step.

Constructive destruction is one of the most delightful employments in the world.

Joyce Maxtone Graham, author of *Mrs Miniver* under the pen-name Jan Struther

1
The wall

- ❏ I am right and you are wrong

- ❏ My world

- ❏ The prejudice barrier

- ❏ What's stopping me?

- ❏ Amanda's story – there's an opportunity in there somewhere!

At the beginning of this book we used the analogy of opportunities being placed on one side of a wall while we stand on the other side. And of course, while we stand on the other side it can be tempting to see the wall as an insurmountable barrier. In this chapter we look at how we can break the wall down. In particular we concentrate on:

1 The restrictive seeing of opportunity that inaccurate self-perception can create in us.

2 The wall that is built when we believe that certain kinds of opportunities are taken by certain kinds of people for example, entrepreneurs are extrovert.

3 Believing that we are right and therefore discounting anything that doesn't fit the rightness of our argument or opinion.

4 Turning negative reasons for not taking an opportunity into positive justifications for taking the necessary actions.

■ I am right and you are wrong

You might have some terrific personal attributes but be using them in such a way that you are restricting your capacity to spot and take opportunities. When we make assumptions about our personality traits, we respond to opportunities that we feel are best suited to our personality. But our self-image is often based on our life experiences to date. For example, we may have had a bad experience at work or perhaps even earlier at school, and that experience may have caused us to make assumptions about ourselves based on how we reacted in that situation.

Assumptions about our personality can also make us see the world in limited ways – even if those personality traits are admirable. For example, most of us like to believe that we are intelligent. But there are dangers in this. If we hold a particular view in our head, we say to ourselves that our view must be correct because we are intelligent and have reached our conclusion because we have reasoned the argument in our own mind. If this were true, then all intelligent people would hold the same opinions and world view. In politics, where a high number of 'intelligent' people reside, there would be no such thing as right and left wing.

To be an OST, a suppleness of mind may help us to see the world in different ways. The more we are able to adopt a range of perspectives and mindsets the better able we are to see our way out of a problem or to see opportunity where more limited thinkers are seeing only one dimension in any given situation. Rigid, fixed thinking can mean that we approach problems and opportunities with 'in-built' inflexibility.

Good examples exist within the world of science. Most of us would consider those in scientific pursuits to be 'intelligent'. And yet even in this most 'intelligent' environment, we have an almost endless number of examples of rigid thinking slowing down the pace of scientific advancement – the 'old way' of thinking refusing to entertain new ideas. If we go back in history, we can see the outcry created when Copernicus suggested that the Earth might be going round the Sun. When the head of IBM once suggested that the world would need only five computers, many bowed to his superior knowledge. Sometimes the experts can get it wrong. They should at least expect to be challenged!

We are perennially fascinated by the potential for life beyond Earth. But we are told that life will exist only where there is water, because water is essential to support life. Within our current understanding of what constitutes life, that is true, but we may discover one day that it isn't. Holding this view may antagonize those with scientific knowledge (which I freely admit I don't have) right up to the point where we find it to be true. Perhaps ultimately science may prove this notion to be wrong, but it should also allow for the possibility that it could be right – of course, good science does allow for this, it's the closed scientific mind that doesn't. By denying this possibility we build a wall around an avenue of possible opportunity.

What science has shown is that what one generation conceives as impossible, another generation sees as a norm. It gets to the heart of our desire to challenge and explore, that we should seek to do this. But this isn't just an issue about generation gaps. As a race we are always questioning, challenging, disproving, improving and doing these things within our own generation. You come up with an idea, float it among a few friends, and within minutes you have a plethora of new thinking. Entertain new ideas – don't immediately dismiss them. The new idea of today is the opportunity of tomorrow.

■ My world

How do you see your world? A simple exercise is to write down a list of opinions, views and perceptions of the way the world is that are, or could be, held by other people – people whom you disagree with. Politics, music and sport are rich sources here.

When you have your list, try to imagine yourself as the other person and justify the opinion that person holds. Better still is to do this with a friend and pick something that you disagree about. Then have a discussion where you seek to justify each other's position. What sometimes happens here is that we take the extreme position that we think the other person holds.

An example might be something that has occupied many minds in recent years – the war in Iraq that began in 2003. If we believe the invasion to have been wrong but have to justify it in discussion with someone who thinks it was right (but in this situation has to argue against it), we often find our arguments become more extreme as the discussion goes on. This is because we tend to stereotype the person according to the arguments they give. This is why someone who is right wing will tend to stereotype someone who is even moderately left of centre as a card-carrying, high-tax, renationalization socialist, and the left winger will look for Genghis Khan-like qualities in the right winger, ignoring all the things that would disprove this. In our Iraq war discussion, it can be tempting to portray those with a different perspective as somehow extreme.

So what has this got to do with opportunities? Well, it is simply that a more flexible, open-minded view of the world and the people in it can help us in two ways:

1 We bring people into our world that we had previously shut out. Other people bring us opportunities through their thoughts and actions.
2 If we dismiss that which we don't immediately understand, then we won't investigate the possibilities in other arguments. As we have already noted, possibilities create opportunities.

We tend to take seriously the people who hold similar views to us. And in a world where successfully taking opportunities will depend on our relationships with other people, we will need to embrace a far greater spectrum of society than may currently be the case. Entrepreneurs and managers, for example, will not get very far if they surround themselves with a large number of like-thinking individuals. We need a breadth of thinking and ideas to choose from as we continue to identify future opportunities. We saw the need for this in 'The download' in Part One.

■ The prejudice barrier

When it comes to opportunity, prejudice will also create a wall for us. This works in two ways:

1 My restrictions

If a woman believes that organizations are against putting women into senior management positions or on the board, she may compromise her ambition because she believes the goal is unobtainable. In this situation the highly capable woman will therefore not try to attain the senior management position. And of course the result is that if enough women believe this then we get the reality we have – not enough women in senior positions in our organizations. There is considerable evidence to suggest that there is indeed bias against women in senior management roles even in the 21st century. But the situation will not be improved unless women seek to knock down this barrier. Happily, there is significant evidence that this is happening.

So the lesson here is that if we believe something to be an absolute truth, we may be tempted to reinforce that as a truth through our behaviour.

2 My restrictions on others

The second way it works is a challenge to society, and it says that if we hold prejudicial views relating to race or gender then we are immediately compromising our capacity to spot and take opportunities. This is a considerable barrier to progress. If we believe that sections of our society are inferior to us (and this is what prejudice is), we dismiss a huge chunk of the population – if we are prejudiced against women, for example, we immediately discount the value of 50 per cent of people. We have a moral imperative to champion gender equality, but there is also a practical imperative.

Believe the evidence – an exercise

I've suggested that if we believe ourselves to have certain characteristics, we are inclined to behave in the way we associate with those characteristics. But how accurate is our self-perception? Write down some examples of personality traits that you see in yourself. Don't write down only those things that you find undesirable or, conversely, desirable. Your list may include qualities such as:

- Shy
- Introverted
- Positive
- Lacking in confidence
- Cheerful
- Hard-working
- Prone to laziness

Your list will clearly be longer than this. Put a star against those characteristics that you believe hold you back. When you have done this, immediately look for examples where you showed the opposite character trait to the one starred. We all have a unique mix of behaviours within us and we can all find examples of situations where our behaviour contradicts our self-image.

The key here is that, while this self-perception may be right, if it isn't we may shut out opportunities that fit the stereotypical image we have in our heads of people who take these kinds of opportunities. We need to challenge that stereotype too. If we believe that only extroverts are entrepreneurs (the Donald Trump type) then we will tell ourselves that we can't be entrepreneurial if we don't fit this stereotype. This is of course nonsense. Some of the best public speakers, for example, are very shy in normal circumstances but are able to bring out this other self when they make a presentation. The reason we don't think we can be an introverted low-profile entrepreneur is that we are unlikely to hear about them for precisely that reason. But they exist everywhere.

It may be that we have been operating in environments that have not allowed us to express ourselves in the way we would have wanted. The undesirable straitjacket restricts us to a limited expression of our true selves. Could it be that if we believe the straitjacket to be a fact of life, then we will explore opportunities only if they fit into the perception we have of ourselves, even if it is inaccurate?

Don't be trapped by your own self-perception! Seek to challenge it.

■ What's stopping me?

Many readers around the world will have enjoyed the TV programme '15' where British celebrity chef Jamie Oliver took 15 young people from tough backgrounds and trained them to cook so that they would become chefs in his soon-to-be-opened high quality restaurant in London. Most of the 15 young people had personal issues that were creating problems. Jamie Oliver took them on knowing the 'personalities' involved but nonetheless trained them so that they could be high-class chefs.

The programme excited the so-called 'chattering classes' and the broadsheet newspapers because, in their eyes, it confirmed their view of the work-shy young being presented with great opportunities but choosing to reject the chances they are given. In a sense this view was understandable. The programme tended to concentrate on those who let a succession of personal issues get in the way of taking the opportunity they had been given. What the programme and indeed other commentators chose to downplay were the 50 per cent of the group of 15 who had actually grabbed the opportunity with both hands and were getting on with the job of being highly capable chefs trained by one of the country's leading professionals. What a marvellous thing to be able to say for the rest of your life.

The success stories in this, even though some of them had their own problems outside the kitchen, had decided to have a go – to knock down the wall preventing them from going for it. Of course, part of the skill of taking opportunities is to take the ones that are right for us – 'know yourself' – and the law of averages says that some of the 15 would be totally unsuited to the job of chef. It also became clear that there were some trainees who were finding less than valid reasons to throw away the chance they had been given. But the abiding memory of a fascinating experiment has to be the 50 per cent who saw the opportunity for what it was. It would be interesting to see how the 15 end up in say, 15 years' time.

In another environment altogether, the 2005 hurricane Katrina in New Orleans produced an interesting reaction in some of those who chose not to go back to the city after the clean-up. Having lived in one of America's toughest and poorest cities and to an extent having become 'institutionalized' by that environment, many people were suddenly given a glimpse of a different world and were not overly keen to go back to the old one. Some decided to see the chance of opportunity in adversity and took the decision to carve a new life in new surroundings. It became a chance to start again. The very real 'wall' of displacement from home became the opportunity to try something new.

These are not meant to be trite arguments. This is not an insensitive exhortation 'to pull yourself together' when confronting great personal difficulties. It is merely meant to say that in times of personal difficulty our best chance of recovery may come in looking for opportunities in the new circumstances. Where perhaps we make some kind of personal resolution that will propel us forward in those circumstances. Even if our circumstances aren't compromised, it is easier to find reasons not to do something than to action the one compelling reason to do it.

Why not try this? Ask yourself what opportunities you are working on at the moment. Search for the single most persuasive reason to action it or them. Write it at the top of a blank sheet of paper. Then list the reasons why you have doubts. Then ask which of these are actually valid. That is to say, which of these has no way out – the immovable brick in the wall. For each of the bricks then try to find at least five ways to overcome the difficulty. For example, imagine if we are considering changing jobs, the compelling reason to do so may be:

'This is now the time in my life when I need a new challenge. Without it my life is in danger of becoming very stale.'

We might find the following things are holding us back:

1 Better the devil you know than the devil you don't.

2 I might not like my new job.

3 Why risk what I have now?

4 I am good at this job.

5 I have good friends here.

OK, so now present arguments against this. I've presented some counter arguments for each of the points below, but before you read on try to come up with some of your own.

1 Why should the next job be the devil? It assumes that all jobs have inherent evil within them! Believing that something could be bad makes it more likely to be so.

2 You might not. But going in thinking you might not is hardly the best way to start. Again you are more likely to create your own reality if you think this.

3 There is always an element of risk when we take any opportunity. But if we don't take any risks then we at best stand still, at worst, go backwards.

4 And you'll be good at the next one too.

5 And if they are good friends you'll keep them. And make new friends too.

Amanda's story – there's an opportunity in there somewhere!

I was and still am in a stressful job. I work with people who really need the help of social services – many struggle to do the most basic things mainly due to drug and alcohol abuse. And I have to admit that at times I just wanted to say to some of them, 'Snap out of it – look at my life.' I work full-time and I have four children aged between 8 and 18. For a long time, and I am sure many parents will recognize this, I tried to juggle all the balls and I found myself with a lack of 'me' time. I'd get home at about 5 pm and it was straight into the world of cooking, cleaning, children and so on.

I didn't feel like I was the only person in the world in that situation – I knew there were plenty of other people including work colleagues who were in the same position. What made me different was that I began to try and see if there was a way to get a bit of 'me' time. I must admit that, in my worst moments, I had flashes of 'I've had enough' but in the end I made a tough decision. When I describe it, it sounds rather brutal but in reality it isn't like that at all!

I gathered my family together and told them that after 8 pm it is my time. If they are still up, and of course they are, then that's OK but I'm not cooking, cleaning, washing, ironing or doing anything else other than things for me. Suddenly I had a bit of breathing space. I could do some reading, get on the internet, do a little gardening in the summer which I really enjoy, and generally start to reactivate my brain which was so sterile before. Of course, what happened is that if you stop doing things for people then they realize quite quickly that they have to do it for themselves. I even caught my 16-year-old son doing a bit of his ironing before he went out one evening! I think my family respect me for it. I started doing an evening class once a week, studying French – I have to leave before 8 for that – and I feel a bit liberated as a result.

It hasn't reduced my effectiveness as a mother one bit. What it has done is given me an opportunity to freshen myself up – to take an opportunity to enjoy a bit of leisure time that I didn't believe existed. I think it's made me a better person at work too. I'm less grumpy and a bit more balanced as a result. I've injected some perspective into my life.

Where can you apply the wrecking ball in your own life? Is there a way through or over the wall that you are missing?

Old walls need knocking down?

Never see the sun?

Can't see the wood for the trees?

Too much to do, too little time?

Always looking for excuses?

**Knock down the barriers – change the world
forever with the help of:**

The
Wrecking Ball
Company

What our customers say...

'They did a great job... Berlin has never looked better!'
The Mayor of Berlin

'Your people were terrific. Please thank them.'
The Hitch family, Wallsend, Newcastle

*'Leave my
wall alone!'*
Hadrian

Everything is a risk these days. Every film you make is a risk. Nothing is guaranteed.

Cameron Diaz

2
Terra incognita – unknown land

❏ How high the moon?

❏ Woodworm – risking everything

❏ Do I always have to take risks?

The psychology of taking risks has been one of the hotter topics in psychological study over the last 50 years. And there is no question that to take opportunities we do have to take risks. But why should we take risks when there is no apparent need to do so if we are able to have shelter and feed ourselves? There is considerable evidence to suggest that taking risks is a primeval instinct. When we evolved from ape-like creatures we lived in a very dangerous world with predators around us that were far more threatening than any animal now known to us. But to sit in the cave meant to starve. So we had to venture out, with all the dangers and risks to life that this held for us. It seems that even though the brain has evolved considerably since that time, its stimulus that prompts us to take risks has survived.

We all take risks all the time. Crossing the road is a risk. So is eating a meal out. So is changing jobs. So is climbing a mountain or getting on an aeroplane. If we didn't, we would not have evolved to the point we have reached. It is just that some of us are prepared to take greater risks than others. With most of the more mundane risks we take, we have at some point calculated that the benefit of the action we want to take outweighs the risk contained in the action. We cross the road even though there is a minute risk of getting run over, because we see advantages in getting to the other side – the shop is there, our friend lives there and so on.

But things get a little more interesting when we look at the kinds of risk that people are prepared to take. Some of us are prepared to risk our lives to a considerable degree to get the thrill or the 'high' associated with the risk. Others, perhaps the less inhibited, like to take risks of a more exhibitionist nature. But what is certainly true is that although some of us are clearly risk averse, we all recognize the need to take at least some risk. As Shaun Edwards, the celebrated rugby player and coach, has recently said:

The biggest risk you can take is to take no risk.

The question is: how much? The greatest opportunity takers are also the greatest risk takers because in every opportunity we take there is the risk of failure. But to use a well-worn cliché, what is the failure?

1 Never trying and therefore never having invited the possibility of success?
Or

2 Trying and perhaps not getting the level of success that you imagined?

To help you work out your thoughts, you could draw up a chart with four columns. In the first column, list some of the opportunities that you could consider taking in your life. Think about things such as asking someone out, changing jobs, starting a business or even moving to another country. In the second column, list as many of the possible gains that you can think of for each possible opportunity. In the third column, do the same thing for possible losses. What is significant is how often we underestimate the possible gains because there are so many potential unknowables, based around the new people we meet and the first-time experiences associated with a new environment that stimulate our thinking. We underestimate the gains because we are moving into an as yet unknown world – so the fourth column can include an element of fantasy: where could the opportunity really take you?

As far as losses are concerned we can be a little more certain (but not absolutely!) about what these might be. The risk of changing jobs is that you won't like the new one, for example. But you probably left the old one because you were getting a bit stale anyway. So how much were you losing in reality? The person you were asking out could say no. But hey – as good-looking as you are, not everybody is going to love you! Dented ego yes, but not forever. Moving abroad risks the loss of contact with friends and family, and the reality that your familiarity and comfort with one set of rules and laws means nothing in a new country! All that built-up knowledge just hanging there but now unusable. But these are not calamitous losses if we balance them against the possibilities that a new culture might offer us.

Because the losses are easier to calculate, it can become easier to talk ourselves out of something than talk ourselves into it. Even though we 'kind of know' that the opportunity might enrich our lives, our risk averse head takes over and we might be inclined not to go for it. If we are to spot and take opportunities, we need to keep an open mind about what the benefits might be. In your thinking, allow for a raft of possible avenues that could open up for you. Think creatively about this. The arc of possibilities is likely to widen if we take the chance. The arc of loss is unlikely to grow significantly into uncharted waters unless we are very unlucky or are taking what we might call a very stupid risk.

■ How high the moon?

So taking risks is important to the OST. The phrase 'thinking the unthinkable' has become part of the lexicon of governmental and business thinking and once got a government minister (Frank Field, MP for Birkenhead, Liverpool) the sack when he did precisely this with healthcare and the government didn't like what he said. A classic case of 'I like the thinking but not the thought!'

Just thinking and offering opinions can be risky to both reputation and career. So taking risks requires a little bravery!

Why not try this? If you have difficulties taking risks, try and answer the following two questions in this order:

1 What risks could I take in the next 12 months?
2 What might I be missing out on if I don't?

■ Woodworm – risking everything

The Company Woodworm makes cricket bats. But they haven't been making cricket bats for very long, only since 2001. When your potential competitors have been doing this for a hundred years it's difficult to know how to compete. Do you start small and chip away at the big company's market share and hope they don't really notice until you are a major competitor (a surprisingly successful tactic)? Do you go for a niche within the market and grow from there – special lower cost bats for the weekend player rather than the professional? Or do you go bang and risk everything in an all-out attack on the market leaders?

These were the dilemmas facing Woodworm – a start-up business in 2001 whose partners had secured £1 million of venture capital. A good start, but also one loaded with danger with such high stakes involved. They decided to forgo the protocol of steady year-on-year growth and went all out to muscle their way on to the top table. They looked around the world at the top players and decided that they would sign someone just embarking on their international career who had the potential to be a superstar – they signed Andrew 'Freddie' Flintoff to endorse and use their cricket bats for £250,000. A quarter of their investment budget blown in one go! And they followed it up by signing the almost completely unknown Kevin Pietersen to endorse and use their bats too. Another chunk of the start-up capital gone.

Four years later Freddie Flintoff had become a superstar of the game, famous to those who don't know one end of a cricket bat from the other. Kevin Pietersen is not far behind him in the celebrity stakes – attracting super models and vast amounts of publicity in the tabloid press.

It's all very well having celebrities on the books but the critical factor is – how has it affected sales? The answer is that at the time of writing Woodworm has gained 10 per cent of the UK market in four years and an association with two of the biggest global superstars of the game. They have done it with only five full-time staff – outsourcing everything they can to outside companies. They are trebling turnover every year.

But there was another risk that the company had to take. They needed something to make the bat look distinctive. The founder of the company, John Sillett, had borrowed his father's very own bat for a weekend game but had had to shave off the woodworm-infested edges. He scored 142 runs with it in one game (for the benefit of American readers, that's like scoring three home runs in a baseball game). He noticed, even though the bat was weighty, that it had a very light 'pick-up' which meant it was more comfortable to use when playing the big shots (the type of game that both Freddie Flintoff and Kevin Pietersen like to play).

Key points

How high is the moon?

In a version of one of the classic sayings about taking risks, it is possible to believe that it can be better to aim at the moon and reach the top of the sky than to aim at the sky and hit the ground. Often we find that our achievements may only match the sum of our aspirations. Risk takers as a rule have high aspirations. There is little point in taking big risks when we perceive few practical benefits in doing so. At the beginning of this chapter we looked at the need that all of us have to take risks. Our curiosity and our desire for exploration in part fuel this desire to take risks. But risk taking is not really about just running on a flight of fancy. Risk taking can have elements based in intuition and instinct and other elements based in hard-headed realism. Combine the two and match them to your aspirations and you may find the opportunity you saw opening up into something much bigger.

Woodworm took a huge risk with considerable sums at stake. Even though the risk was huge, it wasn't stupid. They very carefully thought out whom they were going to ask to endorse their bats. Their decision was not based on an ill-thought whim. Even the biggest risks need not be a throw-away decision. We can think big and still be realistic.

A combination of bravery and realism may get you well beyond the moon and heading for the stars! It certainly seems that a combination of bravado and intuition has created a very successful business for Woodworm.

■ Do I always have to take risks?

No, and Woodworm didn't risk everything. On the one hand they risked a lot by signing potential future stars to endorse their product, particularly Freddie Flintoff. But on the other hand they are very shrewd in keeping the number of employees to an absolute minimum – with bat production being done by outside companies in Cambridge, England and Bombay. From interviews with the managing director, it is very clear that in all other aspects of their business they are extremely prudent.

They also recognize that 'brand image' is everything. To today's consumer, the product is often less important than the image the brand name evokes. A touch cynical maybe, but nonetheless in this image-conscious age a start-up business would do well to consider the image it wants to project and then gear itself towards creating that image. There are risks here in that the image you project may not reflect the aspirations of the customer. But getting charismatic and successful young sports people to endorse your product is a sure-fire way to capture the hearts of the younger generation. Woodworm used a combination of bravado and intuition to make a critical decision that would make or break their business. But the intuition of the partners told them that although they were taking big risks, these risks were tempered by using a format that had worked well in other business environments.

Only the stupidest of mice would hide in a cat's ear. But only the wisest of cats would think of looking there.

Roger von Oech

3

Change your conditioner

❏ In from the outside

❏ Global eating habits

❏ Selective seeing

How does it feel to be an outsider? Some of us feel uncomfortable because our upbringing has infused us with a series of social norms, values and conventions that we unquestioningly carry with us. These things that we carry and are most comfortable with may be the ones that are useful in our new environment – where we are now the outsider. But some of us like the fact that things are different – we are able to stand outside the new environment and see it for what it is. We are not wrapped up in the conventions of our new surroundings and as a result may be more able to spot opportunities in places where others may not even be looking. In this section we seek to challenge existing practices and norms by encouraging readers to apply 'outsider' thinking. Get out of your own conditioning for a while and make a mental note of what you see.

■ In from the outside

This is the story of a man, very sadly no longer with us, who in the 1990s emerged in a country he had never visited before and helped to re-energize what had become a moribund music scene. The country was Brazil and the person's name was Suba. Not many readers will have heard of Suba, but his story tells us a lot about how being an outsider can help to change something. Suba (real name Mitar Subotic) was born in Serbia and became a classically trained musician at the Novi Sad Academy of Arts. Suba left Serbia soon after and moved to Paris where he became increasingly interested in avant-garde sounds, experimenting with electronic sounds in music. While in Paris he was awarded a prize by the UNESCO fund for the promotion of culture in music that included a three-month trip to Brazil to study the musical rhythms of that country. He ended up in the vast multi-ethnic, multi-cultural urban sprawl that is São Paulo (or Sampa as it known by locals).

Anyone with even a basic knowledge of popular music will recognize the huge global contribution that Brazilian singers and songwriters have made to this form. Songwriters such as Antonio Carlos Jobim, Vinicius De Moraes and Jorge Ben have written some of the most popular songs of the 20th century (even if you have never heard of them, you would be surprised to know how many of their songs you recognize). The Brazilian sound pervades many forms of modern, western music.

But Brazilian popular music went through a decline in the late 1980s and early 1990s. It seemed that a vast country that produced some of the most inspiring and recognizable music of the postwar era was unable to re-invent itself and place its traditional sounds and rhythms in a modern context. The music was becoming a poor parody of its old ebullient self.

Suba, as an outsider, could see the vast potential of the music scene and soon began to love the unique musical sound of the country – once described as the perfect mix of 'happy sadness'. But Suba had no real emotional investment in the old way and soon began to bring together the vast array of Brazilian talent and create a new sound using the experiences he had gained in other parts of the world – particularly with the use of electronics and other modern technological innovations.

He kick-started the highly influential music label Zirguiboom (to add to the 'global' story, it is based in Belgium). The 'Brasil2mill' compilation made a massive statement about the direction the new music would take as it featured both new and old stars creating new and exciting sounds. Even though he was carving a new sound, many of the 60s singing stars began to praise the developments in Brazilian music he was inspiring. Where Suba won was that he was able to use the best of the old and the best of the new. He loved and understood Brazilian rhythm but combined these forms with new innovations. Brazilians recognized the old influences but enjoyed the fresh perspective he had brought to them.

In 2000 Suba's own record 'São Paulo Confessions' was released, and has been heralded as a classic – totally justified in an era when the word is applied far too liberally. It is, say critics, one of the handful of most influential albums of the last decade. People started to take notice of this new sound abroad as well. 'Tanto Tempo' by Bebel Gilberto (daughter of 60s stars Astrid and Joao Gilberto), produced by Suba, has become the biggest-selling 'world music' album in the world in the last decade, and he also discovered new singing star Cibelle. New and powerful groups such as Nacao Zumbi and Otto emerged to further move the sound forward and combine electronics and new vocal styles into rock sounds. And a whole new genre of music has been born – Sampa Nova. This is not just the new sound of São Paulo but the new sound of Brazil too.

So how did a Serbian come become so integral to the New Brazilian sound? The answer probably comes in three forms:

1 Suba understood and loved the old sound but he wasn't a part of it

He had nothing personally invested in the old culture – he didn't have to play by the old rules. At the same time Suba caught the zeitgeist. Because he was outside the conventional world of Brazilian music, he was able to stand on the outside and look in. He saw a huge raft of musical talent searching for an outlet. He provided the outlet.

Sometimes we struggle to see opportunity because we are too wrapped up in our own world. When we look outside our own very small world we begin to see greater opportunity.

Why not try this? Make a note of those times when you have thought, 'Why don't they do it like that?' or 'Why hasn't somebody done this?' Sometimes we dismiss those thoughts because we assume somebody has tried it. In reality everyone else is probably thinking and saying the same thing.

2 You don't have to change everything

Many readers will have had the words 'we have to change' thrown at them from governments, employers and the media to the point that we could question every single part of our life if we wanted to. The point is that changing things to make the most of new opportunities (and avoiding stagnation in the old world) does not mean throwing the whole of the past away.

People searching for new career opportunities or organizations looking to change their business model could perhaps begin by building on strengths rather than looking to throw everything out and starting again. Could we use the good things we do as the basis on which to move forward?

For Suba it meant taking the classic Brazilian sound and fusing it with new ways of making music. It didn't mean ignoring Brazil's amazing musical heritage.

3   What have I got to lose?

As someone who had experienced different cultures, Suba was open-minded enough to see that there are a multitude of ways of doing things and he could apply his more worldly view to the situation. The wall that he could have created – 'I can't do this because that's not how Brazilian music sounds' – didn't exist for Suba because he hadn't been institutionalized in the old way. Suba probably didn't even see the barriers that others assumed where insurmountable. So the wall that we build that says 'I can't take this opportunity because I'm an outsider' can be transformed into 'Why not me?'

Why not try this? If you're pondering a problem, ask how an outsider might see it. Try to suspend any prejudice or 'we couldn't do this because' contamination in your thinking. Outsiders won't see what you see as a problem and this will take them in a different direction. Be an outsider on the inside.

Suba died in a house fire in 2000 – apparently trying to save the master tapes for his next record before they burnt in the fire. His peers around the world including great artists from the USA and the UK brought out a record 'Tributo' in honour of a man who made a massive contribution to global music sounds in the very short time he was able to do it.

> Don't discriminate against ideas because they don't fit the old pattern.

'*A breath of fresh air*' – Barry Normal, *The Daily Optimist*
'*This could run and run* * * * * *' – Johnson Rosse, *Film Quarterly*
'It's changed my life forever' – Tommy Blaire, *Dawning Street Courier*

Based on a true story of courage, personal struggle and determination to change the world...

The Outsider

Rated 18R

Showing in an imagination very near you.

A *free* BOTTLE OF NEW 'CONDITIONER'
WITH EVERY TICKET SOLD.

■ Global eating habits

In another example of applying outsider thinking we can look at the change in eating habits around the world – but in particular in the UK. In 30 years London and indeed the rest of the UK has gone from being one of the worst cities in Europe in which to eat out, to being arguably the best in the world – eating in the countryside has been described by Raymond Blanc as superior to doing the same in the world gastro centre, France. A BP *Eating Out in London* guide from the 60s contained the same number of restaurants that it would be possible to find in one street in the present day. What created the revolution in the UK's eating habits? And why had it been so bad for so long? A number of factors changed things.

The British started going abroad on holiday and experienced what they had, for so long, been terrified of – foreign food! At the same time a huge and newly arrived immigrant community, unencumbered by the traditional one-dimensional eating habits of the UK, simply carried on eating what they always had and, more importantly, began to offer it to the native population. Those who offered their cuisine probably never saw any reason why this new food should be rejected – and it wasn't. The idea of eating out and well, traditionally the preserve of the few, became an accessible lifestyle choice for the many. With mass migration now a fact of global life, many other countries have found eating out to be a completely different experience to, say, 20–30 years ago.

The long-term effect has been an awakening of the nation's interest in food to the point where to be a chef is seen as an aspirational career choice for many. The next time you are considering opportunities – whether it's a new career, a business opportunity or a leisure activity – ask yourself if the range of options laid out in front of you is being restricted by your own conditioning. How might someone else view your circumstances?

■ Selective seeing

In *The Day of the Triffids*, one of John Wyndham's characters says this:

> *We must all see, if we pause to think, that one kind of community's virtue may well be another kind of community's crime: that is what is frowned upon here may be considered laudable elsewhere; that customs condemned in one century are condoned in another.*

Notwithstanding these truisms, when we find ourselves living according to an unwritten set of cultural norms, we can start to believe that these norms are the only way of living. As such, we run the risk of seeing opportunity only within a defined set of norms that our familiar culture has set for us.

This perhaps explains why the powerhouse cities of the world – London, New York, Paris – have relied on a continual influx of non-native people to the city to regenerate its creative energy. If, for example, New York relied on indigenous New Yorkers to maintain its creative engine, it would run the risk of grinding to a halt. It's the ability of those who aren't constrained by existing modes of thinking who may bring new approaches, ideas and energies to an environment open-minded enough to absorb them. New inhabitants in those cities aren't wrapped up in the old way. Cultural norms that we absorb as we grow up may affect our judgement in certain circumstances as we revert to what is safe rather than opportunistic.

Why not try this? Take a look at the four pictures below for a few seconds and then close the book. What did you see? Write down what you saw on a separate sheet of paper without looking back at the four pictures.

A version of this exercise originally appeared over 40 years ago in a book called *The Psychology of Perception* by M. D. Vernon. The exercise then was done with a group of children. Half of them were shown each picture in sequence and asked to write down what they saw in each one. The other half were told to look at the four pictures in sequence but had been briefed about the face beforehand. What happened is that the group who had been briefed reported seeing the face for much longer than the group who hadn't been briefed, even though they were allowed the same time.

So what things did you write down? Because you hadn't been briefed, you may have come up with a selection of observations for each one. If you had been briefed about the face, would you have been looking for the face in each one? The point here is that when we are conditioned to see certain things we look only for the things that we are conditioned to recognize. Take the conditioning away and we see much more. An extra dimension to this exercise is that it may also reflect how prone some us can be to come up with obvious, less risky answers to each of the pictures (the bottle in the last one, for instance) because we may be afraid to break out of conventional thinking. Indeed, some us may have seen the bottle but dismissed it because it didn't fit the conditioning we had experienced by looking at the first picture or being told about the face.

Gorilla as opportunity

In his book *Did You Spot the Gorilla?* Dr Richard Wiseman cites a study that took place during a practice session of basketball. Observers were asked to count the number of passes during a 30-second passage of practice between one of the teams. While they were counting, a man dressed up as a gorilla walked on to the court, beat his chest and walked off again. Remarkably, many of the observers, when questioned afterwards, had failed to notice the gorilla.

Of course, having this capacity to concentrate hard on one thing is an admirable human trait and serves us well in many situations, but it also provides the seeds for what we might call 'selective seeing'. Richard Wiseman (wisely!) points out that we often fail to see opportunities in the same way the observers failed to see the gorilla. Sometimes the answers are right in front of us. It's just that we don't see them.

Averting your gaze – faces and gorillas

Our eyes are only one way in which we see. While the previous two examples involve the connection between our visual system and the brain, and our capacity to see more than we are being conditioned to see, there is a link here with opportunity spotting. The longer we are conditioned by our circumstances or institutionalized by our surroundings, the less likely we are to avert our mental gaze in other directions. As someone once said, we often spend so much time watching one door closing that we fail to notice the next one opening.

Opportunities out of nothing

In his very funny book *Eat the Rich*, writer P. J. O'Rourke profiles different countries and in his cynical but very precise way pinpoints what has made them succeed or fail economically, socially and politically. He places Hong Kong as the winner in the 'How To Make Something Out of Nothing' category. Hong Kong has no natural resources, no space, no agriculture and almost nothing else from which you could a believe a successful economy would need to spring. But when I say 'no natural resources' I am being a little disingenuous because it does have the natural resourcefulness of the one thing that can overcome any apparent difficulty – the remarkable energy, drive and capacity for hard work of its people. Just imagine if we magnified that microcosm of capitalist enterprise that is Hong Kong and expanded it into the whole of China with its one billion plus people. What might China begin to look like? This might not be so fanciful because we are starting to witness a giant awakening, the like of which the world has never seen, and our own worlds may start to look very different because of it. And of course, unlike Hong Kong, China does have many 'natural' resources too.

So where do opportunities come in here? There are three powerful lessons that we can take from Hong Kong.

1   Identify your biggest asset

Hong Kong and its people show us that, even if the odds are not stacked in your favour, if you don't have some of the advantages that others may have, you still have that one asset that can take you where you want to get to. That asset is you.

2 Opportunities come through hard work

There is one indivisible truth about both spotting and taking opportunities that the people of Hong Kong show us. And there is one indivisible truth about spotting and taking opportunities that, say, a 90-year-old Italian farmer contentedly looking back at a long life of productivity shows us too. If you want to read a book on opportunities and find some kind of quick fix – something that will allow you to short circuit the often tough path to some kind of personal fulfilment and attainment – then you are unlikely to find it. If you can't be bothered to put in the effort, then the opportunity won't find you or, if it does, you will not be putting yourself in a position to make the most of it. The simple truth is that we cannot get past the need for maximum effort when pursuing our opportunities.

3 Don't be a slave to apathy

I recently worked with a group of people – around 20 of them – and asked each to describe their perfect day. Three identified 'winning the lottery' as that day. I was curious about this and probed a little further. The conversation took, for me, a worrying turn when it seemed that at least two of them were waiting for that day. Everything else that led up to that moment was some kind of preparation for the inevitable lottery winning nirvana. We cannot sit here and criticize this perspective because each has their own perspective on life. But all I can say to those who have this armchair mentality (it might not be winning the lottery, it might be an inner voice that says, 'I am waiting for an opportunity to find me') is that you might be waiting a very long time.

Part of the conditioning that we get in wealthier countries leads to the eighth deadly sin – the onset of apathy. What the example of Hong Kong shows us is that even with little in our favour we can create so much more than might be immediately apparent. Think of what we could achieve when we have so many of the odds stacked in our favour. With the opportunities we have, we cannot complain that we never had the breaks when we didn't do very much to get the breaks in the first place.

Bad things are not the worst thing that can happen to us. NOTHING is the worst thing that can happen to us.

Richard Bach

4
Great success from minor disaster!

❏ Education

❏ Opportunity to test yourself

❏ Did you get on your bike then? Being made redundant

There are many things in life that can make us think that we have failed, but there are two in particular that can leave us feeling shattered: not getting the expected grades at school-leaving age, and being made redundant. The first causes a big problem in industrial societies where we are placed under huge pressures to succeed educationally, while losing our job seems to make our world collapse around us. When things don't quite work out for us or when setbacks in life send us down paths we haven't previously conceived of, it can be tempting to see ourselves as failures.

■ Education

Some of your friends will no doubt glide through life on a moving platform of A grades and first class honours degrees. But look at it this way: you've had the unexpected chance to get off the conveyor belt, to look around you and discover what else life might have to offer…sometimes as you look you will find opportunity in unexpected places.
Journalist Roland White in the *Sunday Times*

Western societies are going through a period of radical experimentation with their young as they seek to encourage increasing numbers of teenagers to continue education and go to university. No bad thing, of course, to encourage 'education' – but the exasperation clearly felt by many of those who do not get the required grades is worrying. Those who leave school at 16 or who didn't get the grades for college or university can be made to feel like failures. But we can respond to our circumstances in any way we choose. We can of course try again next year with the determination and belief that this time we will get it right. To do this we need a cool, rational look at where we went wrong this time.

This is just a simple lesson about honesty. Think of a situation where an opportunity that you took didn't work out for you. What were the reasons for it? Did you give it your best shot? Did you put in your maximum effort? Was it right for you anyway? Sometimes things do happen that knock us back. The failure is often a necessary part of the success we seek. What is key here is how you respond if things didn't work out for you. How you respond when you arrive into the world without qualifications or qualifications that fell below your expectations.

If your response is 'Try a bit harder next time' or 'What can I learn from that experience that I can use to my benefit next time?' then you are recognizing that next time it will be your effort that makes the difference. You are taking personal responsibility for your future circumstances (remember the '4 Rs' on page 72). Disappointments or failures should not be used as a stick to trash yourself with. Failure is a necessary part of future success. It is a necessary part of life itself.

But this piece is really aimed at those who, for whatever reason, didn't fulfil their expectation or get the grades to move into further education. Many people are not suited to learning in the formal way we are taught at school, and failing at school is not a reflection of stupidity or incompetence. And of course, education and learning come in many forms – university being only one of many vehicles for them.

■ Opportunity to test yourself

The point here is that, as our *Sunday Times* journalist suggests, no matter what form your failure may take, there are a million and one other things you can do and opportunities you can take.

If you want to flower, you can flower. Just don't assume that the flower that comes out will be the one you expect. It, and you, could be an entirely new species! However, in times of perceived failure, lying dormant and expecting the world of opportunity to come to you is unrealistic. Like all seeds, you need to nourish yourself and find the environment in which you can flower.

And to go back to our original point about the pressure to undertake further education and get a degree – if we end up with a society where 50–60 per cent of the annual newcomers in the workforce have a degree, employers and indeed society as a whole will have to look at other factors to distinguish between people. That's where you come in if you are one of the people without one! But at any time the limits on what you can try are born only out of lack of imagination and will.

I can get ahead

The workplace can be a great leveller. Unless someone's degree or further qualification is directly vocational, those of us without one can find that the three-year advantage we have over others can pay dividends in the workplace. We can see it as a head-start if we want to see it that way. By the age of around 26 many of these qualifications become irrelevant as we learn that what guarantees success in life is energy, commitment and initiative. These are things for which there is no formal exam. Unless you see life as an exam! And of course as we go through recognizing that we may need to upgrade our knowledge and skills, we can re-educate ourselves. But this time we are doing it with a greater level of personal motivation and in a subject where we know we have an interest. Many of us are not mature enough at 18 to make those decisions.

Do it your way

It seems almost fatuous to produce a list of great achievers who left school with no qualifications, but many of our great innovators, entrepreneurs, business people and political leaders have come through with no academic qualifications. Anita Roddick, Richard Branson and Jamie Oliver are all people who left school with no qualifications. Great writers have emerged with none of the obvious literary qualifications. But our achievers share key character traits.

1 They have high expectations about life itself – even if they choose not to express themselves through the academic route.

2 They have a 'can do' spirit. They are self-confident and committed and believe that what makes a person successful is the positive approach they bring to life.

3 They don't see themselves as lacking in intelligence. It is just that they have found a different outlet to express it.

This is not an excuse to justify the actions of those who think it is 'cool' to duck out of school, but more a plea to those who didn't get the qualifications they wanted to realize that your life is only just beginning and there are a million and one ways in which you can express yourself to the world – you just need to work to find those things.

■ Did you get on your bike then? Being made redundant

In the 1980s British politician Norman Tebbit got lambasted by sections of the press for advising the unemployed not to sit around all day and instead do what his father did in the 1930s depression: 'He got on his bike and looked for work.' It was a tough message at a tough time when 3 million people were out of work and where redundancy had become the common currency of failing industries. Norman Tebbit was not a man noted for subtlety and the way the message came across indicated a kind of contempt for those who were unemployed for any length of time. But the sentiment, that nothing happens to those who do nothing, had some sense to it.

As we move deeper into the 21st century it is said that being made redundant will become a fact of life for many of us. Public sector workers, who perhaps entered the world of work believing they had a job for life, can clearly no longer have this expectation. Some organizations strip whole layers of management in the name of efficiency or to satisfy the needs of shareholders and the redundant get left behind.

But perhaps, in his less than sensitive way, Norman Tebbit was on to something. How do we respond when redundancy in particular chooses to visit us? For many readers this will be a reality. If we find ourselves being made redundant it can be hard to see where the opportunity lies in a situation where we may feel like failures. Here are some key factors to consider – they will work just as well for you if you are still employed but looking for new career opportunities:

1 Get yourself into a positive mindset

There are a million and one ways to leave your employer and this is just one of them. You left your employer.

At what is a tough time you must tell yourself that redundancy is not a reflection of your capabilities. These days employers take a non-human perspective. In an age where people are seen as 'human resources' rather than 'human beings' organizations recruit on the small number of proven competencies required to fill that job. If your job role is no longer required, employers don't necessarily look at the human being involved – at the personality – they look at the competencies. There might be only five, six or seven required. If, as I am now asking you to do, you list your capabilities, you should be able to come up with 10–20. Finding it tough? Think seriously about it, because recognizing your capabilities will be one of the first steps in rebuilding your confidence during this tough time.

Just because you have one or two competencies missing from the list of five, six or seven required by your previous employer does not mean that the hundreds of capabilities you have inside you will not be of use to other employers – or indeed to the wider world in another form. Perhaps it's time to start that business you've always wanted to run.

2   Cast your net wide

Do not categorize yourself. It can be very annoying to hear people describe themselves as an 'unemployed lorry driver' or an 'unemployed sales rep', almost saying that this is the only thing they are capable of doing. Tell yourself that you are unemployed (temporarily). You are not an unemployed …(fill in previous job).

Think about the times when you meet someone new: the first question we usually ask is 'What do you do for a living?' This is understandable – as human beings we have a desire to categorize or stereotype. But regardless of whether you are currently working or have been made redundant, move your mindset away from this restrictive self-categorization. Your mindset should be 'I can do this. But I can do many other things too.'

If you have a limited view of your capabilities, everyone else will too. Do you really want to tell the world that you can do only one thing? Is redundancy the opportunity you've secretly cherished to go and do something else? The opportunity hasn't come in the manner and at a time of your choosing, but they rarely arrive that way. And if you are stale in your current job and are seeking a move, these mindsets will work equally for you too.

3   Adopt the campaign mentality

It's an old saying, but nonetheless a true one, that if something is worth doing it is worth doing properly. Looking for new job opportunities isn't a casual walk in the park. Look at this way. You've lots of free time to prepare the next chapter in your life. Why not write 50–100 applications a week to prospective employers? Two or three just won't be enough. And why not make a few of the applications for roles that are outside your current comfort zone – don't dismiss something because it hasn't hit your personal radar before. What have you got to lose?

Better still, phone around. Imagine yourself as the cold caller selling something. They always say that the best sales people are the ones who sell something they care about. And do you care about you?

4   I can do that

A feature in this book is the knocking down walls mentality of the opportunity taker. Instead of finding reasons why you can't do things, look for good reasons why you can. If, for example, you are a housewife or househusband who has been bringing up children for 20 years, then you have myriad skills that employers would welcome. Think about the time you organized a children's party. Was it not a formidable feat of planning, controlling large numbers of people? Use your experiences in life in a positive way. Employers value that positivity when they are comparing you to others.

The bricks in the wall are all self-imposed reasons why you can't do things. Knock them down one by one.

5   This could be the best thing that ever happened to me

Our disposition in tough circumstances may be the key variable here. If we behave like this is the worst thing that ever happened to us, people will pick up our negative disposition and it is likely to reduce the level of proactivity needed to get the most out of this unplanned-for situation. We should not feel embarrassed about redundancy and we should not articulate this embarrassment to future employers. In the same way, at future interviews we should talk positively about our previous employer – even if we still harbour much anger.

In the modern world, the need to negotiate the spider's web that is the modern organization, means that career paths are no longer linear. Can you learn to treat the change as a positive move forward in your life rather than an insurmountable hurdle? You might not be doing the thing that you wanted to do, but apply a positive mindset to your new circumstances and you might find that the change was exactly what you needed.

This could be a fantastic chance to do something completely different.

6 Harsh realities can breed new opportunities

At the time of writing we live in an ageist society that values youth over experience. This may change as organizations recognize the value of experience, particularly in people skills, and because western societies have ageing populations and will need to draw on a different age profile for their employees. But at the moment, to be made redundant in your 50s can be very serious because of the reluctance of employers to recruit from this age group.

However there are still great opportunities. Many in their 50s do get good jobs and many do say that they never realized what a rut they were in until they were forced into looking for something new – but the campaign mentality recommended in point 3 applies here. Other opportunities exist too. Many in their 50s, for example, consider the possibility of buying a franchise. It gives a sense of control over one's own business at a time when redundancy can leave us feeling that we no longer have this control. Others will look at the possibility of starting a small business – all those years of experience can now reap benefits for you.

The true way to render age vigorous is to prolong the youth of the mind.

Samuel Taylor-Coleridge

5
The third age

❑ Ann's story

❑ Creating opportunity in the third age

❑ Why the sudden jump?

❑ Daphne's story

When my eldest daughter was about three years old we spent a lot of the weekends together because my partner was working. Rather than do the usual things like going to the park or sitting indoors and drawing or painting, we would often go to the free lunchtime concerts held at London's South Bank Centre every Sunday. The music used to vary from jazz to big band sounds right on out to more esoteric manifestations of global music. All the music was fairly upbeat and very danceable. I must confess the first time we went was a spur of the moment thing and I wasn't really sure because I thought my daughter might be a bit bored. And of course I had filled my head with what I perceived our trip would be like. I perceived, correctly as it happens, that it might be aimed at older groups.

When we arrived my perception was immediately shattered. The place was packed – around 500 people. And yes, the age profile was probably 55–80 years old. My completely prejudiced mind had said that this was likely to be a fairly sober occasion – lots of polite clapping in the right places and a gin and tonic that would last three hours. How wrong I was! This was a rip-roaring, get stuck in, strut your funky stuff lunchtime extravaganza! The bar was packed, the dancing committed and the applause for the musicians wildly appreciative. My daughter loved it too, dancing away with people 20 times her age. We went back many more times and I always left with more energy than I arrived with – always a good sign that leisure is serving its purpose of mental reinvigoration.

I now have a slightly different view on what retirement means. What exactly are we supposed to be retiring from? Work perhaps – but certainly not from occupation. And most definitely not from knowing when and how to enjoy ourselves! But there are many ways to live a fulfilling, enjoyable third age, as Ann's story now illustrates.

Ann's story

I was born in 1923. I had a good childhood and spent the war training as a nurse at the London Hospital in Whitechapel and continued working as a staff nurse and then a ward sister until 1951.

After this I spent the next 21 years being a full time mother to my children, wife to my husband and daughter to my elderly parents but even then I suppose I was thinking about expanding my education. I managed to do a diploma in Sociology and a German O level which stimulated my interest in study – something I would go back to later in life. I had been offered a place at University College, London, in the early 1950s but I hadn't quite gained the required equivalent of A levels, but the desire to get a degree didn't leave me, even though I had a home to run. University wasn't really considered an option after I had left school.

I returned to the world of paid work in 1975 working as a voluntary services co-ordinator with social services. I retired in 1984.

With four children all having degrees as well as my husband (who died two years ago, but who is always with me), I suppose I may have felt a little left behind. But I didn't see it as something unattainable. I knew that I would go back to it. And so in retirement I did.

It came about, I must confess, as a suggestion from someone else in the office I was working in just before retirement (a little nudge is sometimes all we need!). But I was really seizing an opportunity that had been denied me earlier. I started a degree course at the Open University in the UK in 1982 and finally graduated in 1989. One of the modules on my degree course was 'Historical Sources and the Social Scientist' and that module in particular had captured my imagination. So I decided to follow it up with a post-grad diploma in English local history at what is now Portsmouth University. When I finished my dissertation for the diploma, I thought I could add to it and give it another life in book form. So *Shere Poverty* on the subject of the poor law in the parish of Shere was published by me and has sold well for a book of that type. The senior librarian was very supportive of me, and certainly didn't see my age as a barrier!

I became even keener to develop my areas of interest, becoming a member of the Local History Society and having another small book published on the history of a local tannery – at one time the biggest employer in the area. Encouraged by this, I was bold enough to tackle my biggest project yet together with my husband and my brother. In the First World War, my father was in the Territorial Army and was sent first to India, from there to Mesopotamia and then to Egypt and Palestine. He had no home leave and didn't get back until January 1920. During all this time he wrote to his fiancée, later my mother. All his letters survived, and we transcribed them and annotated them and my brother wrote introductions and I published them under my imprint. I think it is good! The book was called *Engaged in War* and it was published in 1999. I continue my work with the Local History Society and love responding to the queries and questions we get through our website. I continue to enrol in courses when something really captures my interest.

So what makes me do the things I do? Interest plays a part. I'm curious too. I find out about something and I want to know more. I must say that you do need some measure of self-belief to go for things and the support of others is very important too. I did find opportunities popping up for me at the right time, but I think my curiosity and interest in things, and the fact that I was prepared to dig a bit to find out more, created those opportunities for me anyway. If I had spent my retirement doing nothing, what opportunities would have come my way? I do remember not particularly enjoying reaching 60 – it seemed at that time to represent the end of professionalism – but retirement certainly hasn't been like that for me. I would never preach to anyone about retirement and all of our circumstances are different, but I do think that retirement should be seen as an opportunity to do new things. Retirement for me has not been a time when I stop setting the alarm clock in the morning!

To me at least there seems to be a large amount of material advising on how to enjoy retirement. Much of it is one-dimensional and seems to indicate that all third agers will want to spend their time joining clubs and societies and doing good works for the local community. At its worst some of this material has a frightening 'try and keep yourself alive' feel to it. It's almost as though retirement should be seen as a battle against the inevitable. One way to bring on the inevitable is to be thinking about it all the time! Pursuing retirement opportunities means going for the things we like doing because we like doing them, not because we think we should. The answers to a fulfilled retirement are the same as the answers to a fulfilled life, but they will be unique to you because you are unique!

It seems that above all else this is an opportunity really to start to enjoy all the things we have always enjoyed but with the added ingredient that we now have the time to do them. In addition to this we now have the time to explore new opportunities, when before we were wrapped up in the world of work and family.

■ Creating opportunity in the third age

So here are three key general points that may help to create opportunity in the third age. They don't apply just to retirement of course, and repeat some of the points made elsewhere in this book, but they do provide a useful trigger to a proactive and fulfilled third age.

Curiosity

It is said that when we get past the age of 40, our life starts accelerating away from us. What makes earlier life stick out in the mind more is that many of the things that happen to us are happening for the first time. They become memorable for that reason. As we get older, many of the things we do we find we have done many times before and as a result they are less memorable. And so the argument goes, as we have less memorable experiences later in life our life speeds up because there is less that stands out for us.

But of course, this isn't true for all of us. And neither should that be the reality. Perhaps the key here is to maintain curiosity and to seek more memorable first-time experiences. This is a version of what we might call 'playing time'. In the same way that what makes childhood so memorable is that we have so much time to play, explore and experiment, the argument goes that in the third age the same thing applies too – as Coleridge suggests in the quote on page 126, 'prolonging the youth of the mind'. One of the interesting points about Ann's story, as she says herself, is that her curiosity is one of the things that is fuelling her in retirement. First of all she allowed her imagination to be captured. And once that happens we find ourselves becoming more and more involved in the thing that has called us. But we have to want to hear the calling!

Capability

As in pre-retirement, we place a major restriction on opportunity if we respond only to those things that we have done already. And yet we hear wonderful stories of those in the third age who are discovering things about their true capabilities that they had never imagined before.

A simple exercise highlighted earlier bears repeating here: list five things that you believe you are capable of – and look closely at your list before you read on. Ask yourself how many of these reflect things that you have already done, that is, things that are provable. Many of us will have five provable things on our list and will be tempted to live our lives according to those past achievements. These past achievements are important – we can use past successes as confidence builders. But it can be helpful to add 'capabilities yet to be explored' as a way of building a positive, explorative sense of the future.

There is no reason why, in retirement, we cannot continue to stretch ourselves and explore new possibilities. When we continue to explore, we find that we can do things, regardless of age, that we had not previously imagined.

Spontaneity

One of the dangers of prescribing potential solutions to anything is that if we live our lives according to a set strategy we cut down the possibility of spontaneity in our lives. If we analyse many of the case studies in this book we see how many opportunities come from impulsive reactions. Sometimes it happens that the more we think about doing something, the more inclined we are to talk ourselves out of doing it. Sometimes it can be exciting just to go ahead and do what we were thinking of.

■ Why the sudden jump?

When we reach the third age it can be useful to think what our needs might be. Human beings of any age need occupation. It's just that in the second age our occupation is either work or running a home. Some carry on working through retirement, and a number of organizations are offering the chance to ease into retirement by reducing the number of days worked over a period of time.

The change for some can be a shock – from a full-time job to no job in the space of a couple of days. Some readers may benefit by making the gradual move between the two rather than the sudden one. It allows us a bit of time to think about what our needs in retirement may be, and to start to develop the things that have always been part of our lives but can now come to the forefront.

We place a huge amount of pressure on ourselves by building up the word 'retirement'. It's almost as though a mythical thing will happen but, like anything else, to maximize its enjoyment we have to work at it. Some of us become psychologically retired many years before we actually stop working, seeing life as one big drudge – almost as though we are counting the clock down. I wonder if this mindset prepares us for what lies ahead. What a dreadful waste of valuable 'living time' that must be. As in life itself, retirement doesn't happen to us – we happen to retirement.

> *Retirement for me has not been a time when I stop setting the alarm clock in the mornings.*
> Ann Noyes

Ann's story tells us a lot about a positive, opportunity taking mindset in retirement itself. What about the lead-in to retirement? Do we have to jump from full-time occupation into a complete change of lifestyle? Daphne's story illustrates the value some of us might get from carrying on – particularly if we love what we do.

Daphne's story

From the age of 20 right up until the age of almost 60 I brought up children. I had my first child when I was 20 and then in my late 30s I had two more. None were planned but I enjoyed being a mum and I think I was good at it. I had to bring up my two later children by myself and money was always very tight. As you can imagine, the opportunities to work were restricted because of my role as a full-time single mum – I did lots of cleaning jobs to bring in extra money.

As I reached my late 50s and my children were leaving home I had to think more about my future – the switch from thinking about your children all the time to thinking about yourself is a big one, but suddenly I had a bit of time. I started working in a nursing home and got my first ever qualification – a National Vocational Qualification – that allowed me to 'nurse' a little more and do some of the things I didn't enjoy so much a little less! Two years on and I'm feeling like I'm doing something I probably always knew I could but never did.

I suppose you could see this as a sad story. Yes, I could have seized this opportunity at a younger age. But then again, I could easily have gone through my life without finding out what was right for me. I think the bigger sadness is that so many of us never find out our vocation in life. I think I always knew there was a side of me that enjoyed caring for others and now I have been able to do it. I am very happy about that. I don't see the point in regretting what I didn't do. I am just thrilled to be doing something I really enjoy. I have to say it – 'I LOVE MY JOB!' I am nearly 60 now and I have to have a regular health check to make sure I am OK to carry on working – I understand that. But I see absolutely no reason why I should stop until I have to. I'm occupied, stimulated and fulfilled. Why retire from that?

The choice is simple. You can either let life melt by not doing the things you wanted to do or you can decide to play.

Entrepreneurs are simply those who understand that there is little difference between obstacle and opportunity and are able to turn both to their advantage.

Machiavelli

6
Open for business

❏ Starting a business

Consider the mid 1990s. No one would deny that out of technological advances came the most spectacular opportunities for internet entrepreneurs. And yet, amid this burst of innovation and opportunity came horror stories of people losing millions (and in the case of Marconi, billions) in real money or in company valuation – this was particularly true of established companies and of banks lending money irresponsibly to ill-thought-out start-ups. How could this happen? And what hope is there for others when they see apparent experts getting it so badly wrong?

1 Many bigger businesses tried to move into markets they didn't understand with methods of working that failed to reflect the demands of new customers. Some didn't actually know what they were doing but thought it might be fashionable to pretend they did.

2 Many start-ups floundered because they thought that a good website would be all that it would take to pull in the advertisers. Massive risks were taken on the assumption that advertisers would jump on board websites where customers were not paying for the services they used.

3 Established businesses were too locked into the old way to be able to respond to technological advances. The new kids on the block, Amazon and eBay for example, had no investment in the old way. They came in with fresh clean thinking.

These are all lessons that contemporary businesses can learn from – particularly when markets and market paradigms change quickly. The technological revolution continues and the lessons from those early days are still relevant. But now let's leave failure behind and assess what it was that made some of the world-famous brand names that didn't even exist 15 years ago. What can we learn from them?

The idea of selling books through the internet seems logical with hindsight and seemed like a good idea at the time too. We could all understand why we might not actually need to walk to the bookshop, and the logic of saving time by having a book delivered to your door. Even then, however, some bravery was required on Amazon's part. We were being told that the internet would kill off the book because we would be all reading 'on screen' or downloading and printing off our choice of reading. And this may become a reality in the future – Stephen King has published 'web only' material.

Amazon also had to absorb huge financial losses in the early days, leaving a lesson for all business entrepreneurs:

1   Do some scenario thinking

What would you do if your future financial projections were, say, a year or even two years premature? Do you have a fall-back position? How might you change your business model if you had to? Could you secure further investment if you needed it?

eBay provides us with a powerful lesson for start-ups and for established businesses looking at new markets.

2   Reassure customers

The model that eBay was working towards seemed to have more risk. Internet auctions? The idea may not be so risky, but in the early days customer uncertainty about how this might work must have created the need for the very solid auction sales model they now work with on the site – one that created a relationship of trust between buyer and seller. I remember asking myself, 'How can I be sure I will get my goods?' 'What if my goods aren't quite as seen and described on the site?'

eBay, recognizing these crucial issues, developed a feedback system that helped to create a relationship of trust between buyer and seller to the point where at the time of writing only 1 in 10,000 transactions are found to be fraudulent in a sales environment that could be open to abuse.

Such is its popularity that books are now being written on some of the things that have been successfully sold on the site (Glastonbury mud £400! 20 UK pence for £1!). And many will be aware that old rope does indeed sell – as in 'money for old rope'!

There is a strong lesson here about customer reassurance – particularly when a new business is being launched. Entrepreneurs need to work hard to get those early adopters – as consumers, we say, 'You're new, can I trust you?' Like those travellers sailing off in the 1500s and 1600s to discover the new world, they prepare the ground by which others will follow. Only when someone shouts back, 'It's safe out here' do others then begin to do the same. It needs the early uptake of a few pioneer customers to prepare the ground for your second wave of customers to follow. You can have the best ideas in the world but as a start-up – or even if you are introducing a new product and service – if people don't trust you they won't go with you. Work hard to build that trust and do it quickly.

■ Starting a business

When we start a business we seek to provide something that:

1 People never imagined they wanted and then when you provide it they can't imagine how they did without it. For a time the iPod and a succession of 'me too' mp3 players hit this niche. The internet is a classic modern-day example.

2 Others provide but which we provide better. Better and more personal service, speed of service and better quality of product or service win here. Five restaurants sit next to each other in your local high street. Which one do you pick and why?

3 Turns the convention of a product or service on its head and provides it in a new way. Simon Woodruffe and his Yo! Sushi chain hit on the idea of providing food on a conveyor belt (although this wasn't his idea, he popularized it) around which we sit with our fellow diners and pick off the dishes we want. We like eating out. Yo! Sushi provides a novel way of doing it.

Readers of an entrepreneurial persuasion may be attracted to the creative aspects of all three of these. Here are some suggestions that can help you come up with new and creative ideas for business opportunities. Try mentally wrestling with the following questions to stimulate your thinking:

1 What don't people have the time for?

Or perhaps another question – what things do people still do for themselves that they would pay someone else to do? Thirty years ago most of us still took our lunch to work. Now most of us buy it while we are at work. Thirty years ago most of us cleaned our car with a bucket of water on a Sunday morning. Now a big machine does it at the local petrol station. Or some entrepreneurial types do it at my local Safeway car park while I am shopping.

Amazon understands that many people don't have the time or inclination to go to a bookshop and have responded to that.

2 What don't people like doing?

Think about some of the tasks that you have to do but don't like doing.

- Searching for the best financial deals (so we go to a financial adviser)
- Unblocking the drains (so we pay large sums for someone else to do it)
- Exercise (so we buy stomach reducing belts, diet meals and a variety of tablets)

What don't you like doing that no one is currently offering to do for you? Is filling that gap the opportunity you are seeking?

3 What makes me different? What can I offer?

Can you tell the truth about yourself truthfully? What I mean is – are you able to define accurately the things you are capable of (trying the exercise on page 132 may help you to see your capabilities in a new light). Most of us dramatically underestimate the things of which we are capable. And most of us barely begin to explore the extent to which we can stretch ourselves. Those that do report a remarkable level of personal fulfilment in their lives compared to those who just tread water.

What you can offer will be dependent on another factor. Think about your existing level of provable skills. And when you do this do not underestimate current or previous achievements. Parenting, for example, offers a whole raft of skills that begins with organizational skills and teaching skills and carries on to an almost limitless demonstration of highly desirable attributes. When we begin to understand what we are truly capable of, or when we want to test out what our level of capability really is – that's when we begin to explore the never-ending list of opportunities available to us at a deeper level.

Have you got a talent or a particular interest you could capitalize on? Do you have a leisure interest that could move to the centre of your life – both for income and for time spent doing it? I can recall meeting a man who spent much of his spare time repairing the old TVs and radios of friends. He became an expert in the internal workings of most major brands' products. And he would frequently stay up till 3 or 4 in the morning immersed in wires and strange gadgetry. What a great opportunity to have a fulfilling 'cottage' business.

How you view yourself will be particularly important as you assess what kind of business you want to develop. Do you want to run a small business or do you want to be an entrepreneur? Although there are considerable similarities, there are differences too, as shown below:

■ **Amount and speed of wealth creation** A small business may generate substantial wealth but will do so at a slower speed than the entrepreneur – possibly over a lifetime. The entrepreneur seeks to move quickly and to generate substantial profits with a shortened time frame.

■ **Risk** All business start-ups and expansions require risk. Because entrepreneurs want to buck trends (both in speed and wealth creation) they will be prepared to take the greater risks. They will often pursue the unknown with the intention of turning that unknown into the norm as quickly as possible.

■ **Innovation** Entrepreneurs like to move quickly, certainly more quickly than the average market growth of the chosen industry sector would allow. To do this may require a substantial amount of innovation that may be beyond the norm for a small business. The innovation may come through the product or service itself, or the systems and procedures that bring that product or service to market.

Decide what you want to be, because it will determine the type of business you establish – and, as attractive as being an entrepreneur sounds, it will not suit every personality type.

4 What could be done?

In Part One I mentioned futurologist Joel Barker and his work on paradigm paralysis – being blinded to the future by the routine of the present. In his writings he presents an antidote. He offers us what he calls the paradigm shift question:

'What is it impossible to do now, but if it could be done would fundamentally change the way we do things?'

These paradigm shift questions have been asked throughout history, but especially so since the onset of the Industrial Revolution. We find, however, that many established organizations with the rigidity of their 'This is the way we do it' thinking are disinclined to break out of conventional thinking modes.

Asking the paradigm shift question takes us closer to bringing about the reality of what we perceive to be impossible. The word 'impossible' is ambiguous. It means it is impossible to do with current modes (paradigms) of thinking, but, change the way we see the problem or opportunity, and suddenly the impossible becomes possible – and remember: right at the beginning of this book we defined opportunity as the *possibility* of doing something.

We witnessed a great paradigm shift at the turn of the 20th century. It had long been a human ambition to be able to fly, and new technologies were allowing inventors to explore the possibility of flying machines. The trouble was that these inventors and engineers were locked into the idea that any flying machine would have to flap its wings like a bird. Many readers have probably seen some of the hilarious black and white film footage of various terrifying contraptions trying to get off the ground. The paradigm shift in thinking occurred when someone suggested flying machines with fixed wings that didn't flap.

Perhaps, with the huge increase in the numbers of people flying and the ever-decreasing amount of fuel available, the next flying paradigm we will have to break is the one that assumes that planes run on kerosene – the fuel that currently 'drives' aeroplanes.

These are big subjects and it can be easy to ignore how practical the paradigm shift question can be on a much smaller, personal level. Start examining some of the everyday problems that we confront, and try to challenge some of the assumptions we are making about the problem or about the opportunity. Paradigm shifts work equally for us as workers. We make assumptions about the job we do and the jobs we are capable of doing and rubber-stamp our capabilities on our forehead because of it. But in truth there is no reason why we cannot widen the scope of employment opportunities if we ask the paradigm shift question about our own lives.

5 Look back

> *Just because something doesn't do what you planned it to do*
> *in the first place doesn't mean it's useless.*
> Thomas Edison

Current opportunities can happen for us when we look back and assess what's happened in the past. Think of pioneers who first went to the moon or to Antarctica. A number of people went to Antarctica at the turn of the 20th century, but then it was left unexplored until the 1950s because technology had not moved as quickly as the human imagination and too many lives were being lost. We now have a permanent base there. The same applies to the race to get to the moon. After the initial expedition there with Armstrong, Aldrin and Glenn, a whole spate of moon landings followed. No one has been there since 1972 and only now is moon exploration about to restart. We've learned from the experiences and mistakes from the first time round and now have a greater understanding of what to expect and what the opportunities for scientific discovery might be when we go back again.

The person who said 'Don't look back' may not always be right. The lessons from the past can sometimes create the opportunities of tomorrow.

Think about more mundane things. We now take television for granted, but in the 1970s many homes (including mine for a time) didn't have one. What if we could watch whatever TV programme we wanted at any time at the press of a button? Someone asked that question a few years ago (when it was impossible to do) but in a very short time it has become close to reality.

6 'Wouldn't it be great if…'

'Wouldn't it be great if…' is another version of the paradigm shift question.

We produce masses of rubbish but in this environmentally aware time we know that we can't just keep on dumping it and expect it miraculously to disappear underground. And with the time pressures we have we do not have the time to go the municipal tip. Along comes a company. 'Any Junk', who for a small fee will come and take your junk, sort through it, recycle what can be reused, give useful things to charity shops and get rid of what is genuine waste. So Any Junk are answering that 'Wouldn't it be great if someone would just take my rubbish away' question by doing just that. And we keep our conscience clear at the same time.

7 Marketing

When I was small and five
I found a pencil sharpener alive!
He lay in lonely grasses
Looking for work.
I bought a pencil for him
He ate and ate until all that was
Left was a pile of wood dust
It was the happiest pencil sharpener
I ever had.
Spike Milligan

In the spirit of trying to do what your potential competitors are not, here is some advice to help market the product or service you offer. Conventional marketing says that you should gear your marketing at your customer by addressing their aspirations and concerns. Express your marketing and your selling points in language your potential customers will relate to.

But marketing also offers a wonderful chance to use the 'creative download' we talked about in Part One. Why not try a little marketing that comes from left field? Think about your product or service from its point of view. Imagine that it were a real living, breathing thing. How could you make it more attractive? What would it say if it could talk? How might it sell itself?

Did Spike Milligan's poem make you think, even for a second, about a pencil sharpener of your very own? Did it make you think if you had one or not? These are the first steps we take before we go out and buy one. So it must be working! If we send subliminal signals that we love the service or product we offer, or that it has very human qualities, then our potential customers are likely to notice.

We can have the most original business idea in the world but it is irrelevant if no one knows about it. Use that great brain that produced the original idea to come up with great ways of marketing what you do.

With quick hand pluck at the fruit which passes you by.

Ovid, ancient Latin poet

7
Fruit picking

❏ Mary and Doug Perkins – a lesson for entrepreneurs

❏ Chinese military strategy

❏ Robin's story

S ome opportunities are open to us for our whole lives. As we have seen, we also have the capacity to create opportunities for ourselves out of our imaginations and this ability stays with us for our whole life too. However, there is a third group of opportunities. These are the ones that may exist for only a short period of time – and they are often the ones we identify, decide not to act on and then say 'I wish I had…'

■ Mary and Doug Perkins – a lesson for entrepreneurs

Not many people will have heard of Mary and Doug Perkins. In the age of the celebrity entrepreneur, it's curious that two people who get on with the job of running a business that turns over £700–800 million a year and own the business outright themselves should not be higher profile. Their business is called Specsavers. It is the UK's biggest chain of opticians and close to that in the Netherlands and Scandinavia. Using high-profile marketing campaigns, it has built up a remarkably strong brand that is the largest privately owned chain of opticians in Europe. Specsavers commands over 30 per cent of the UK market alone.

As they both near retirement age, Mary and Doug Perkins show no sign of slowing down. They are doing the same thing for hearing aids that they have done for the retail opticians market and also have plans to do similar things with affordable high street dentistry – now there is a great opportunity!

So what has made them successful and why feature them in a book on opportunities? The answers can be found in the early 1980s.

In 1984 the UK government allowed opticians, solicitors and accountants among others to advertise their services to the general public for the first time. It seems amazing now, but before then an optician's could not even advertise in the window the fact that it took Visa and MasterCard! Mary and Doug Perkins had had previous success with a small chain of opticians in Bristol in the 1960s which they had sold, but now, bored with very premature retirement, they saw the chance to get back into the business again. The loosening of restrictive legislation and deregulating of the market meant that they could now more assertively pursue the idea of high-profile marketing to promote opticians. It's interesting that there had always been a need for glasses and contact lenses and there probably will be for many years to come. Why hadn't established opticians positioned themselves to take advantage of this new situation? There was a 'This isn't the way things are done' mentality hanging over the profession, and to an extent Mary and Doug Perkins still have to ride the flak they get for their expansionist approach.

Being able to see this opportunity when others weren't paying attention allowed them to change the image of the staid local optician into the more populist, and some might say more fashionable, image that the local optician now has. This word 'fashion' is extremely important. To wear a pair of glasses in the 1970s was to be seen to be out of fashion. While Mary and Doug Perkins probably wouldn't claim the credit for turning glasses into fashionable items, they embraced people's desire to wear glasses that looked good on them. They encouraged their staff to refer to customers rather than the old-fashioned 'patients'.

They, in the words of Ovid, 'plucked at the fruit which passed them by' because they were looking for the fruit in the first place. What is particularly pleasing in this story is that it is often said (and it is said in this book too!) that the people who change the way industries work usually come from outside that industry. They are not invested in the old way. In this story Mary and Doug Perkins were trained opticians (and in the case of Mary Perkins had a father who was an optician) and had run a successful operation in the 'old way'. Being invested in the 'old way' need not blind us to the new. We just need to keep looking.

In Part One we looked at the Download phase where we think up ways of making our ideas work in reality. Mary and Doug Perkins had the great idea we identified in Stage 1 – they had spotted the opportunity. What did that opportunity mean in reality? For them it meant devising a very creative way of expanding rapidly. Clearly there are many ways in which this could happen, but Mary and Doug Perkins settled on a system where Specsavers takes an annual management fee based on turnover, but the outlet takes the profit. This is seen as joint venture, a sort of 'helping hand', but stops well short of the franchise model that other businesses follow. The incentives to succeed for the individual optician are high, because the profit goes directly to them. They get the benefit of the Specsavers name and the profile that brings, together with a major incentive to perform. As Mary Perkins herself has said:

> *It is because of the joint venture partnership that we have been so successful. We did not want to run a chain of opticians so we came up with this.*

Anyone who starts their own business is an opportunity taker. But the truth is that not all start-up businesses will succeed. It may be the opportunity wasn't original enough, or that the business plan wasn't sufficiently thought through. It may be that the execution lacked imagination. Often it is because the start-up came in too late on the opportunity. It's safer when someone else has trodden the path for you, but more people will be on the same path because it is easier to see – it becomes much harder to stand out. The fruit on the tree stays ripe only for so long.

Key points

1 Sometimes the big opportunity is there for only a short time. If you're ready for it and alert to the possibility of new opportunity, you will be best placed to take advantage.

2 Don't feel constrained to follow conventional practices. What could you do that might be a little (or a lot) different?

3 And finally don't think you can't fulfil your dream of running your own business because you don't fit the stereotypical entrepreneur popularized in the press. The only common denominator is commitment and drive and, as we have seen from the example of Mary and Doug Perkins, it can be done in many different ways. Considering the size of their business, Google the words 'Mary Doug Perkins' and you get a surprisingly low number of hits. They do it their way!

■ Chinese military strategy

When taking opportunities of any kind – be it in business, when we are looking for a new career or just trying to catch the zeitgeist of something new and interesting – we can learn something from late-19th-century Chinese military strategy. The Chinese utilized two military tactics:

Xianthi Zhidi – Gaining initiative by striking first
Suzhan Sujue – Fighting a quick battle to force a quick resolution

In the story below we can see an example of how these two tactics can work for us when both spotting and taking opportunities.

Robin's story

I've tried many things in my life. I started out at drama school at the age of 18 and spent ten years acting in large and small-scale productions in Europe. I loved it but as I was pursuing this route I began to understand myself a little better and recognized in me an entrepreneurial trait. What drove me into acting in part in the first place was a recognition that I was not going to be the sort of person who can adapt to office life easily. I am too free spirited for that.

During breaks in acting work I had been doing some driving work for a magazine publisher. Mostly delivering props to photo-shoots at studios. I had to pick up items from shops and PR agencies around town. I got to know some of them very well. Well, I wasn't your average driver although I learned very quickly that van drivers do not conform to the stereotypical image we have of them. I didn't mind the job at all. It freed up some brain space to think about other things I was doing – such as learning lines!

Well, I was drifting along when out of the blue an opportunity presented itself. The magazine publisher decided that it wanted to use van drivers to do this work on a freelance basis – bringing people in to do deliveries when they needed them. This got me thinking. Here was an opportunity to work for myself with a bit of a headstart. I had the contacts at the various magazines. I knew many of the people at the PR agencies. Could I position myself to get this work but this time working for myself? I had to think quickly. I talked to some of the van bookers at the magazine publishers. Would they still use me even though I was no longer working directly for them? Could I raise the money to buy a van? Did I want to be a van driver? Would it mean the end of my acting aspirations?

I didn't necessarily see these questions as barriers but in this situation I needed to be realistic. I decided to move quickly. I got some reassurance from the van bookers and managed at the same time to raise the money for a small van. A friend of mine had a larger van that he rarely used and in the short term I would be able to borrow it when larger items needed moving. Within a week or so I was up and running with my own business.

Things happened quickly after that. I secured some work with a PR agency and started to work for other magazine publishers too. In a year or so I was running between three and five vans per day and I had a small team of drivers working for me on a contractual basis. The friend who had originally lent me his bigger van came in as a partner in the business and we started to work to grow it.

I have to admit that I don't want a great big business with 200 vans out every day! So at that stage I decided to invest some of the profit in land in India, and I have built holiday homes on that land that I will soon be renting out to the public.

I learnt quite a bit about opportunities. There were other em-ployed drivers at the magazine company who didn't see the opportu-nity I did or who decided not to go for it in the way I did. I also learnt that sometimes you have to move very quickly to make the most of the opportunity. I was the man on the inside so I had a window of oppor-tunity that would have been snapped shut by a bigger transport busi-ness if I hadn't moved quickly.

I also think that that taking one opportunity leads on to others. Without that quick move I wouldn't have had the business I now have and I wouldn't have been able to expand into building holiday homes in India. When we let the lid off something everything changes for ever. For me those changes have been personally very fulfilling. The acting didn't finish either. I was able to produce *Macbeth* in our local pub theatre which played to full houses!

Xianthi Zhidi – Gaining initiative by striking first

When time is limited, a signal of intent can be critical. Robin saw the opportunity and signalled to potential customers that he would be very interested in their business. By striking first, he was able to manoeuvre himself ahead of potential future competitors including much larger established businesses. He already had an inside track but so did others, including some of his fellow van drivers, so he had to move quickly.

Suzhan Sujue – Fighting a quick battle to force a quick resolution

This tactic comes in three parts:

1 Assess the situation.
2 Identify a moment of opportunity in the situation.
3 Develop a quick action strategy that makes the most of the situation.

If we assess Robin's actions, we can see that he responded well to the tactic. He was able to rationally assess the situation accurately and identify the opportunity that existed for him. And his action strategy – talking to potential clients to see if they were happy to use his service on a contractual basis; raising the money to buy a new van; having a contingency plan should he need larger vehicles – meant that at the critical moment he was able to maximize the opportunity available to him.

When we look at some of those life-defining moments (LDMs) we identified in Part One, we begin to see just how often we take opportunities with what appear to be almost impulsive actions. But rarely are they completely impulsive, at least not the LDMs that you define as successful! The need to act quickly, weighing up the actions and then moving into top gear, can often show us at our best as we recognize the potential in the situation. This can be an exciting time, where emotions are heightened and sometimes those emotions can stop us making cool, rational decisions. But the pressure can help us to hone our thinking if we recognize the need to do this. It will be the quality of the action strategy that will determine your success or not. Preparation is crucial but we sometimes need to prepare in double-quick time.

Sometimes if you take the lid off the tin you find you can't get it back on again. Even if you wanted to.

8
One thing leads to another...

❏ Gazmend's story – planning for the future

❏ Andy Cave – tuning in to 'time off'

In Part One we looked at the opportunity curve (see page 26). On the curve we talked about the dangers of resting on your laurels when things are apparently going well for you. The dangers are that circumstances change and because you are in the comfort zone you fail to notice the changes around you. When you see the need to change it may be too late. In this section, we look at Gazmend, a native of Kosovo, as he recognizes the dangers of living on only one opportunity curve line. And in our second case study we feature mountaineer and former coal miner Andy Cave who built a new life for himself from what had been a hobby.

■ Gazmend's story – planning for the future

Gazmend lives in Pristina, the capital city of Kosovo. His main job is to work for the OSCE (Organization for Security and Co-operation in Europe). The OSCE is the world's biggest security organization. Its primary role in Kosovo is to rebuild the public institutions there after the 1999 war. This includes building a strong police force, an effective judicial system and a fully functioning democratic electoral system. Great tensions continue to exist between the majority Albanian community and the minority Serbs, which present many challenges in these areas.

Gazmend is part of the team of nationals (he is Kosovar himself) and internationals working hard to bring political stability to the area. The job keeps him busy but he knows it won't last for ever. What happens if Kosovo gets nation status and becomes stable? Would Gazmend's job survive? What happens if the OSCE scale down their actions in Kosovo? Gazmend started to think about preparing for his future – for a time when the role he performs now is no longer needed.

There were a number of options open to him. He could offer his skills to OSCE operations working in difficult situations in other parts of Europe. He could build on his existing education, get newer qualifications and use them in another field. These are options many of his colleagues are pursuing. Or perhaps he could pursue a different route.

Being an observant man, Gazmend noticed that his fellow workers at the OSCE and indeed the members of the police force, UN workers and many local people needed somewhere close by to go for their lunch, so he decided to build (log cabin style) an Italian restaurant that would serve customers pasta and pizza and snacks and drinks too. Gazmend works a conventional eight-hour day but he does grab a one-and-a-half-hour lunch break every day (central European working hours!) and heads straight over the road to supervise the restaurant. For the rest of the day he has others keeping the restaurant going until he can return after work.

In a classic case of mistaken assumptions, I presumed that he was running the restaurant to make money. 'The money is nice,' says Gazmend. 'But the real reason I am doing this is that I know the work of the OSCE will not last for ever. I have to have something else waiting for me for when my main job ends. I will still have my restaurant.'

This is a classic 'breaking the opportunity curve' story. Gazmend is creating the next opportunity for himself while things are apparently comfortable for him in his main profession. But he is realistic. He knows that if he waited to do something two or three years later, perhaps if the OSCE ever decided to reduce its representation in Kosovo, then it may be too late. This way he has created a new opportunity for himself when he *wants* to – not when he *has* to.

Key points
1 Pre-empt change
Pre-empting change allows us to keep greater control of the future. Through his proactive approach Gazmend has created a new opportunity for himself rather than having to respond to a problem imposed on him.

2 Opportunities exist in the toughest places
Circumstances are tough in Kosovo, with up to 70 per cent unemployment and some political instability. Even in these circumstances, opportunities exist for those who look for them.

3 Build momentum
Other opportunities tend to build from the initial opportunity. By taking opportunities we can build momentum as we meet new people, observe

the world from a new perspective and begin to identify future possibilities. Gazmend's observation of others and their needs, and the fact that he had a ready-made clientele who could use his restaurant, presented an opportunity for him.

In this story Gazmend is building on his current successes and making a conscious decision to plan for the future. Out of one thing he is building another. He is growing his next opportunity curve. In the next case study we are going to look at someone who, through his desire to make use of his 'free' time, grew a new career opportunity curve even though he wasn't aware of it. His name is Andy Cave and he is one of the world's great mountaineers. But he wasn't always a mountaineer…

■ Andy Cave – tuning in to 'time off'

It's the north of England in 1984. One of the traditional industries of the north, coal mining, faces the threat of almost complete closure as the government of the day contemplates shutting down many coal mines. The miners go on strike and one of the most bitter periods in British industrial relations follows as both the government and the miners refuse to give in. Police and miners fight on the picket lines, and families struggle to feed themselves.

Andy Cave worked at one of the most well-known collieries, the Grimethorpe, and lived through this less than happy time. His father and grandfather had both been coal miners before him. It was the life that most young men moved into when they reached working age in that part of the world. What made Andy Cave different was that he had also developed another considerable interest. At weekends and when the mine was out of action due to the strikes, he started to venture out into the Peak District to do some rock climbing. Other strikers went out too. But Andy Cave noticed that he had a flair for climbing as he went on an incredible learning curve during the strike itself. He had found the time to develop his skills and he made use of it.

The strike ended and Andy Cave went back to work but this time with something that was pulling him away from a life underground. He learnt about routes on mountains ('the lines') while reading with his miner's lamp underground. The decision to leave mining was still a tough one, in spite of the lure of life higher above ground than he was below it. Finally he left and the very first season he spent in the Alps. Andy also started to educate himself, taking A levels and eventually ending up with a PhD in Socio-linguistics. He supplemented his income with building work – his above-ground skills coming in very handy – and at the same time he took on tougher and tougher climbing challenges.

Only a few years after leaving mining Andy had become one of the world's leading climbers, establishing new routes on some of the world's great mountains. But then came the challenge that would pitch him into the pantheon of great climbers if he could complete it – the north face of Changabang in the Himalayas. He and three other climbers, including his best friend Brendan Murphy, were to be the first people to try to climb it through this route.

Andy Cave had left a tough existence for another – from miner to world-class mountaineer in a few years. He had found his purpose in life. He had found a level of capability in his hobby that had convinced him to make it his vocation. But at this critical moment he had learnt about the brutality of his calling. They made the summit, half-starved, having survived the harshest of weather conditions. On their way down his friend was killed in an avalanche. 'Was it worth it?' is a question we could ask for ever. But as Andy Cave said himself in a newspaper interview, he once met one of the best climbers of all, Jerzy Kukucka, who said to him, 'Better to be in the mountains thinking of God, than in a church thinking of the mountains.'

Key points

1 Growing the mental hinterland

Too many of us, when we get wrapped in work, forget about creating our 'mental hinterland' – the breathing space we create in our lives when we take on outside interests. The mental hinterland provides a powerful psychological resource for us when things get tough in our everyday working lives. Andy Cave himself called his autobiography *Learning to Breathe*.

2 Using 'down time'

The temptation to waste down time is easy to understand. Rest is good for us. But sloth is not. We can't complain that we never had any opportunities when we didn't get off the sofa and try a few things.

3 Learning doesn't stop when you leave school

Many of us have regrets about not working at school. Many of us say, 'I am going to evening classes' or 'I am going to study for a degree' in adulthood. We haven't focused on Andy Cave's PhD here but we can use it as an inspiration. We can re-educate ourselves at any age, at very low cost. How many of us seriously consider it?

4 Turning on to 'time off'

To some of us the idea of turning our time-off activity into our vocation would kill off the very reason we enjoy it in the first place. Others, however, love the idea of turning hobbies and leisure activities into a full-time occupation. One thing is for certain. If you don't develop your use of time off and develop interests outside your current job, you never get to make the choice.

Why not try this? Make a list of those things that have engaged you during your life. They may not be things you actively pursue now but they may be things in which you have invested some of your emotional capital in the past and which you may go back to. Of course these things may not define a future career for you (unlike Andy Cave) but they may become a central part of your life – and who knows where you may go from there!

The things that truly engage us are the things that make us feel almost as though we are on some kind of holiday. The difference is that this holiday is prolonged, active and achievement-based, whereas most tend to be short and passive.

Build up momentum

We all have a preference for the pace at which we live our lives. Some of us like to live on an almost continual adrenaline rush as we move from one opportunity to the next. Some of us prefer to move at a slower pace.

Have a look at the major things going on in your life. Look back at those times when you felt a real momentum building around what you were doing. Perhaps it was a hobby that had engaged you (like Andy Cave) or maybe you were progressing in your career. Perhaps you were a parent who got into the 'flow' of parenthood. Where do the opportunities lie for you to build your own momentum? What hobbies, interests, career moves or family experiences could help build momentum for you?

One way of building momentum is to use your positive experiences in one aspect of your life to feed into another part of it. Think of how a piece of ivy, once established on a wall, quickly spreads out with branches creating a new division of sub branches. Where is your piece of ivy?

Giving energy and life to your dreams places them in the realm of possibility rather than implausibility.

9

Capturing the imagination

❏ Bernice – a dream come true

❏ Kath Joy – what might it take to get to the Olympics?

❏ Key points from our case studies

Remember those life-defining moments? Or what we call LDMs? Did you make a note of some of them? Have a look at your list again. What made them so significant? What did you do that made them so important? Did you find that your imagination was captured and continues to be captured by something that happened or something you did?

The more experiences we seek throughout our life, the more likely that our imagination will be captured by at least one of them. The more likely it is that we will attain that feeling of truly 'being alive'. In this section I feature the stories of two women who had their imagination captured. For one it happened at the age of nine, for the other it happened at the age of 26. As we see elsewhere in this book (82-year-old Ann, pages 128–130) your imagination can be captured at any age. But you've got to want it to be captured – to put yourself in a position where things start to happen for you.

■ Bernice – a dream come true

Some say that to have dreams means to be naive about the realities of the cruel, harsh modern world. Some say that to have dreams means to be forever disappointed. Some say that to have dreams means to be a fantasist. But sometimes to have dreams means to be alive to the fact we really can do the things we want to if we want to do them enough. And this means to be alive to the possibility of opportunity rather than blind to it.

Bernice Moran was born in Dublin in 1976. Her father had dreams too. He wanted to work for an airline and fulfilled his dream by working for the cargo division of Aer Lingus. At a very young age Bernice pleaded with her father to take her to Dublin Airport to see the planes. As she says herself, 'I wasn't interested in dolls and the things that girls were meant to like. I wanted models of aeroplanes!'

Bernice's brother, seven years older, had his imagination captured too. At the age of 17 he became the youngest person in Ireland to hold a pilot's licence. Bernice went up in the aeroplanes with him when she was ten years old and wanted to fly too. She got, as she says, 'the fire in my belly'. She even took the controls!

Life was tough at this time. Bernice's mother died when she was nine and her father had to bring up Bernice and her brother and sister alone. He managed but it meant that there were no flying lessons for Bernice. She wanted to fly but her father needed convincing that she wasn't just copying her brother. He thought she should go to university first.

Bernice graduated from University College Dublin in English Literature and Geography, and on the very day she graduated her father asked her if she still wanted to be a pilot. Bernice's reply was a very definite 'yes'. During her undergraduate years she had been working in the underwear department of a major Dublin store to pay for flying lessons and, seeing her determination, her father agreed to contribute too.

Eight years on and Bernice has been a captain with Ryanair for three years. But she isn't just a captain. She was the youngest female captain of a commercial airline in Europe. Boeing thinks she may be the youngest in the world. She is at the top of her career and thinking about where the world of aviation will take her next. Bernice has had her battles. She says that women are thrilled to have a successful woman piloting their plane and are always congratulating her. Some men, however, find it difficult to accept and she has to win them over with her skill and professionalism. No airline appoints anyone as a captain of an aircraft, let alone someone aged 26, unless they are convinced of their capability. This, remember, is an environment where attention to detail and accuracy mean everything regardless of gender.

Bernice fulfilled a dream. She decided what she wanted to do and went for it and, in answer to the obvious question, she told me she doesn't regret it for a minute.

Bernice had a dream at a very, very young age. Parents reading this can nurture those dreams and help their children. Bernice's father wanted to be sure that his daughter's dream was a very real one and, once convinced, helped her every step of the way. Will you, if you are parents now or parents of the future reading this, help your children with something that has truly captured their imagination? Will you, regardless of your age, truly pursue something that has caught your imagination? In this short life so few of us find something that genuinely excites us, that says to us, 'This is you, this is what you are meant to do.' If you find it, don't tell yourself that it isn't really possible. Bernice tells us that dreams can become much more than distant possibilities that we never quite end up doing.

Of course, childhood dreams are an essential part of growing up. We can all remember what we wanted to be when we got older. But for our next story we go to Kath Joy, who has created a dream for herself that shows signs of becoming real for her – at the age of 27. Kath's dream was born when she decided to try something she had never done before. She lived for real that great characteristic of opportunity spotters: they are always willing to try something for the first time. Her story tells us how…

▉ Kath Joy – what might it take to get to the Olympics?

Why do I want to try new things? I just want that feeling of being alive.

Positive Thinking, Positive Action featured a remarkable young woman called Kath Joy. The story is this. At the end of 2003 she entered a TV competition to be one of eight chosen contestants to feature in eight different TV programmes where each would have to participate in a physically gruelling race. The idea of each of the eight programmes would be to see if, with a short period of training, members of the public could perform at levels that were the domain of the professionals. Kath got selected as one of the eight to be featured in their own programme and her chosen event would be to participate in the UKATAK.

The UKATAK is the world's most arduous alpine adventure race. It lasts five days, during which participants are required to cross-country ski, snow-shoe (walking in the snow) and bike across relentless snow and ice in freezing conditions. On top of that they could expect to get only about four to five hours' sleep across the five days. Only professionals take part in UKATAK and Kath found herself in a team with three others – all of whom were world class adventure racers. The toughest part was that all team members had to travel together. Slow down and she would slow her team down.

Kath had nine weeks to train for the event from scratch. But a remarkable thing happened. She had set herself the goal of just finishing the race. But as is sometimes the case when we try something new, Kath found out a lot more about herself than she ever imagined. She and her team-mates won the race.

What's more, she also learnt that she had a natural aptitude for cross-country skiing. *Positive Thinking, Positive Action* left Kath's story at that point.

What is Kath doing now? Is she basking in the glory of the win or looking to develop her capabilities? After UKATAK, Kath has had to think seriously about her life. In her professional career she is a very successful brand manager for the huge global business Proctor and Gamble. Things could not be going better. With her aptitude for cross-country skiing, she decided that she would be kicking herself for the rest of her life if she didn't at least try to see how far she can go. Kath continues with her career but at the same time she is training hard in London parks. (You can simulate cross-country skiing training through roller skiing on roads and pathways.) Kath has the goal of the 2010 Winter Olympics in her mind, but she needs to know how realistic the goal is. She knows she has an aptitude for cross-county skiing. Now is the time to test herself. She has entered the British Championships in a 10km race. Finish in the top ten of the British Championships with so little training, holding down a full-time job and against people who live and breathe the snow, then she will know that what is perhaps still a dream suddenly could become a very realistic proposition.

It is truly amazing what we find we are capable of when we try different things. Kath found a hitherto unknown capability for endurance cross-country skiing – to the point where the 2010 Winter Olympics are a very real possibility. The crucial point here is that an almost random decision to enter a TV competition has turned into a very realistic goal of competing for her country in the Olympic Games. It is a remarkable demonstration of how a simple proactive decision can open up a path for us that we could never imagine.

■ Key points from our case studies
Firing the imagination

Both Kath and Bernice in their very different ways illustrate the power that capturing your imagination and, most importantly following it through can get you. Kath's imagination got fired in her twenties. Bernice got the fire in the belly before she was ten. As we see elsewhere in this book, your imagination can be fired at any age. But the fire needs something to help it start to burn. And the firelighters come from you. What interests you? What excites you?

What fires you? What first-time experiences could you try that might provide that first spark? Try something new. Remember that question from Part One: When was the last time you did something for the first time?

Why not me?
Kath and Bernice, in totally different worlds, are fired by a combination of hard-headed realism and self-belief. Opportunity takers combine the two. Bernice recognized the need to knuckle down in a world that requires you to be right first time, every time. At some point the dream fuses into the reality of getting your pilot's licence and the subsequent responsibility for the lives of 200 people. For Kath, it meant testing yourself against the best to see what it might take to get to the Olympics.

Combined with this realism comes a radiating self-belief. Bernice says she never really questioned that she might not reach her dream. Kath believes and says quite openly, without a hint of arrogance, 'I genuinely believe that you can do anything.' They could both have built lots of walls. Bernice was a woman entering a real man's world. Kath was an amateur entering a hard world of professionalism. Both are succeeding and will carry on succeeding.

Why not have a go?
Kath had her imagination captured by taking the very small step of just doing something. Think of those times we say to ourselves:

- I'll try next time
- I am a bit tired tonight
- My chance will come again
- I don't get any lucky breaks
- I never had any opportunities

No one can make you do things. And this book will certainly not be preaching to you about how to live your life. That is your choice. But if you say to yourself, 'I never got the opportunities in life,' it may be because you didn't go out and look for them. It all comes back to personal responsibility in the end. So just ask yourself:

'What can I do that might make a difference?'

The simple hard reality is that no one else can do it for you.

Realism

Your dreams remain just that if you treat them as a 'sitting on a fluffy white cloud' type exercise and don't then attach some hard-headed realism about what is required to make it happen. For Kath it is the hard slog of training while maintaining a full-time job to see if she could be an international class cross-country skier. If she is, then the reality of four years' very hard work up to the 2010 Olympics starts to kick in and the training schedule starts to get really tough. But imagine what the feeling will be like if (and I don't like that word when I refer to Kath!) she achieves her dream.

For Bernice it was the hard graft of working all her free time to pay for flying lessons and of convincing her father that she really did want to do it. She invested much of her childhood and adolescent years pursuing her dream – and she has never regretted it. So when you think about your dreams, get real right away. Ask exactly how you might make this dream become a reality. What real practical steps might you need to take?

Why not try this? Make a note of the things that take up your thinking time. Think of those times when you wake up at 3 am and everything seems so plausible. By the morning we are killing off the inventiveness even though our unconscious has created some new ideas for us. Capture them! Play a little with your dreams. If you were someone else pursuing that dream, how might they go about it?

Can you feel a little well of excitement building up inside you? Are there a few butterflies? If there are, then you might just have taken the first step in making that dream real. If you feel nothing, then maybe you're not being sufficiently fired by your dream to make it something that could be attainable. Desire counts for everything here.

In a wonderland they lie

Dreaming as the days go by

Dreaming as the summers die

Ever drifting down the stream -

Lingering in the golden gleam -

Life, what is it but a dream?

Lewis Carroll, *Through the Looking Glass*

10
Future thinking

❏ Real-life scenario 1

❏ Real-life scenario 2

❏ Be a futurologist

We can all be clairvoyants with a time problem. But what of the future now?

Most of us can recall a time when we said, 'If only…' Someone came up with a great idea and we remember having the same idea ourselves. The difference was that they did something about it. This chapter is about looking forward to see if we can visualize what lies ahead. Readers in business may find it useful as a way of seeing how their products and services may change in the future. Perhaps entrepreneurs will find some way of thinking as a catalyst for their own newly developed products or services.

Will there be opportunities in the future? Of course there will. But the question is: what form will they take? Let's take a glimpse into the future and find out.

■ Real-life scenario 1

Walking around the streets in the major towns and cities of the world can be a hazardous business. We carry so much expensive electronica with us – laptops, mobile phones, mp3 players – that many of us are walking targets for street robbers. One enterprising company saw an opportunity here. They decided to tackle the problem of laptops. It is very obvious when people are carrying laptops – the black laptop-shaped bag is an immediate giveaway. So our enterprising company looked at trying to disguise the laptop. In an excellent example of what we called Neapolitan creative thinking (see page 58) they combined the laptop with something that many people carry around with them – pizza boxes! So now we can buy laptop bags that look like pizza boxes. Even the most enthusiastic street robber is unlikely to risk prison for your pizza. Brilliant!

(Question for creatives – why do laptops look so boring? Why can't we make the laptop look like a pizza? Or like a football? And why can't Apple make a computer look like an apple? There must be an opportunity here!)

■ Real-life scenario 2

England is not a country noted for its apricot harvest. These are fruits usually associated with warmer climes such as the Mediterranean. And yet in 2005 the county of Kent was able to provide a leading UK supermarket chain with enough apricots to stock 250 of its stores. This was the first time that this had happened. What made the difference? The answer lies in the rise in temperature of the last 10–20 years. The result has been that in spring and early summer the county gets enough sunshine to ripen the apricots so that they are suitable for public consumption. In fact their quality has been highly praised. Other farmers are now experimenting with almonds, olives and kiwi fruit to see if they can be grown profitably too.

Perhaps a future of global warming and street muggings is not so exciting but it does illustrate the advantage of open thinking when trying to turn problems into opportunities. So we've had a glimpse of a future. What else might happen? What might the future look like? In the next section we examine some of the more curious possibilities of the near and not-so-near future. As you read it, consider what the impact of some of these things happening would be on your work, your business and indeed your life. And do remember that what seems surreal and perhaps even frightening will seem entirely normal to us in 10–20 years' time. Look at it another way. Think back 20 years and consider what's happened in that time. Are you frightened now?

■ Be a futurologist

So how vivid is your future thinking? David Pearson, Head of Futurology at UK giant telecom BT has predicted that by 2050 we will be able to download our minds into machines. He also says that if you are wealthy, death may not be a serious career move. He believes that the youngsters of today may never have to die. And by extension, the people of yesterday may come back to life. Creepy?

He believes PlayStation 5 will be as powerful as the human brain. And if you happen to be reading this book 10 years on from the year of publication you can decide if he was right!

Here are just three of the other possibilities he envisages by the year 2020:

1 Having a conversation with a strawberry yogurt before you eat it.

2 Chips that fit conveniently in the skin.

3 The linking of nervous systems so that we can shake hands with a person in another room – or another country – and feel the emotion that we would feel if we were in direct physical contact.

Pearson may prove to be right or wrong, and he does of course question the desirability and the ethical dimension of some of these things occurring. His timelines may change but few of us would deny the *possibility* of some of these things happening. The key point here is that, as soon as the human imagination can conceive of something, that person – with someone else if the idea is shared – has taken the first step in making that something become possible. People are working on these things right now. Indeed our own personal microchip may not too far away.

Your imagination need not be so far-future focused or, if you are a doubter, far-fetched. But there is no question that we have the capacity to create new opportunities for ourselves if we can see or create step changes in the way we live. This section makes two absolutely key points, which we will now look at in greater detail.

Key point 1 – I understand what's coming

Thinking about the future can be a horrifying prospect. The predictions we see from the futurology department at BT may not all come true, and the timescales may be a little out with some of them, but nonetheless we can all entertain the possibility that they could exist in the future. So why do so many of us look to the future with apprehension? If we consider the explosion in information technology in the last 20 years and try to imagine a life without it, many of us would struggle to do so. The internet, email, mobile phones with phenomenal computer power and almost real-world gaming are a part of daily life for many. In fact the only frontier that game developers have yet to break though is the creating of a virtual human being that appears to be real. This, game developers acknowledge, is the key breakthrough. And it will come. How do you feel about that? Of course when it does arrive most of us won't even notice, in the same way that the 1990 invention of the worldwide web did not become a reality for the majority for a number of years after that. The pioneers often smooth the path by which the rest of us follow.

And when these things do become a reality, we may struggle for a bit but then we learn to accept technological advances as part of the fabric of living. Sometimes we even become angry at what we missed because we joined in a bit later than maybe we should have. Many internet enthusiasts wish they had 'got netted' ages before they actually did. This is not really a point about slavish devotion to every minor technological gadget and gizmo. It's more a reminder that advances demand our consideration rather than our dismissal. We can't dismiss that which we haven't even attempted to understand.

Perhaps a key lesson for OSTs is an enthusiasm for the future, with all its good and bad points, which makes us much more psychologically prepared to go for opportunities as we see them. For example, did you laugh at the laptop as pizza box story at the beginning of this section, or did it horrify you? Therein may lie the difference between a fear of the future and a willingness to embrace it.

Key point 2 – What's stupid about it?

Today's absurdity is tomorrow's normality. Am I really going to be talking to my yogurt? Could I be having a conversation with Fluffy the pet cat? You might not be, but future generations will, and will consider it perfectly normal. So the key here in generating ideas for opportunities is not to dismiss what seems silly. Remember the word 'silly' meant 'blessed' in the original Anglo-Saxon. So to be silly and to have silly ideas may mean you are blessed with the ability to spot the opportunities of the future! And we can find ourselves making what we call creative coincidence by focusing on the silly part of an idea. It's amazing how an opportunity appears when we think through a 'silly' idea.

For example, think about the historical model for buying aeroplane flights. In the old days the price of flights went down the closer it got to the date of the flight itself. If we booked at the last minute we got a better deal. This changed with the arrival in the US and Europe of lower-cost carriers,

Ryanair for example, who pioneered the idea of the 99 cents/pence flight throughout Europe. The idea of a 99 cents/pence flight was silly – until it happened. Think about how this idea may have become reality. If you ask yourself, 'How could we offer flights from Barcelona to Frankfurt in Germany for 99 cents?' we can work backwards from the opportunity. We might come up with the following ideas:

- Offer a few flights at 99 cents as an incentive to book early
- Don't offer an in-flight meal
- No pre-booked seats – just walk on
- Maximize the number of flights each plane does each day

And in reality this is what happened. So the next time you have a silly idea, ask how you could make it possible. Now other airlines seek to do similar or even the same. The whole model for buying flights has changed throughout the world because of pioneers like SouthWest Airlines and JetBlue in the US and Ryanair and easyJet in Europe. We can now buy cheap flights early rather than just at the last minute. And the last-minute flights of ten years ago were never available at 99 cents anyway.

Entrepreneurs looking to reinvigorate existing markets might like to learn from the example of low-cost carriers. Just take the silly idea and ask how it might be made to happen. Don't dismiss it out of hand. If you are looking for new opportunities in business you don't need to look far to create something entirely new. Sometimes turning an existing business model on its head by seeing a completely different way of doing it will work equally well. Thinking about the future now brings us closer to it.

■ *The past is for learning, the future is for living.* 'Smellovision'
Here's a chance to practise some of those skills we have looked at in this section. One of the great global TV revolutions in the last decade has been the arrival of huge numbers of programmes dedicated to cookery. We live in the era of the celebrity chef – many readers will have seen the lovingly prepared dish on the electronic goldfish bowl and wished they could either smell the aromas they imagine to be easing out of the dish and/or eat it! So perhaps

the holy grail for programme makers will be some sort of 'Smellovision' where we get to enjoy the smell and perhaps eat the dish we see on television. So a simple exercise for you the reader is to think about how you could make this happen. Think about it for a few moments. Out of some of the solutions you come up with could be the opportunity of the near future. And remember the advice in Part One – we are after quantity of ideas, not quality. Get the download working properly.

Here are some ideas that might bring Smellovision closer to reality – but you will have many of your own:

■ Allow viewers to buy all the ingredients in advance so that they can cook along with the chef on the television.

■ Food delivery – phone this number for the delivery of the dish, piping hot and ready to eat, that you have just seen on the television.

■ Scratch and sniff TV guide. Smell the dish that you seen by scratching a strip in the TV guide or in a magazine. A bit like you can with those perfume advertisements in women's magazines.

A note to finish. While writing this piece I heard from a friend of a company looking to develop children's puddings (yogurts and so on) that have a little device in the lid that says hello (rather like those talking birthday cards). How long will it be before we can have a two-way conversation with it?

The past is gone. Is the best yet to come?

I find that the more interested I am in other people, the more interested they are in me.

11
Building relationships

❑ Networking

❑ Valon's story – building relationships

❑ I want to be taken seriously!

Many of our opportunities will come from our interactions with other people. Imagine how our retiree Ann (page 128) would have got on if she hadn't convinced the education authorities of her capability to do her degree. Think about Bernice (page 164) and her need to convince her father that flying for her was not a whim but something she genuinely wanted to do. Or Robin (page 151) and the work he needed to do to convince potential customers that he could provide the service they were looking for.

In many instances the relationship will build over time. You may find yourself developing a strong web of personal and professional contacts through your own skill and expertise. Sometimes, however, we might 'spark' sufficiently with someone so that there is a continual flow of ideas between you early on. In other instances we might find ourselves having to deal with people whom we don't personally like.

In this chapter we look at building stronger relationships that will help the OST. We concentrate on two specific areas:

1 Networking.
2 Getting someone to take you seriously.

Networking

Most of us can think of people we might call great networkers. But we may have different interpretations of what networking means. To some it's those 'working the room' skills loved by politicians and said to be Bill Clinton's greatest personal asset. Others might see it as something more manipulative – building relationships for personal gain. Networking concerns itself with the building of personal and professional relationships – but where the motivation to do so is not built around personal benefit. In his *Networker's Pocketbook*, writer Jon Warner identifies personality types whom we might consider to be 'networkers' by the loosest definition, but only one personality type really reflects what networking actually means:

The user

The user is the person who collects a large number of contacts for personal benefit, with little interest in those people and with little concern for what the other person might get out of the relationship.

The socializer

The socializer prides themselves on a wide circle of friends but attaches little meaning to the relationships, other than the superficial, and therefore has relationships of little substance.

The manipulator

The manipulator, like the user, has little concern for what other people get out of his or her personal relationships, but goes one step further and tries to mould other people around his or her world.

The builder

Our true networker: the builder takes the long-term view of a relationship – not looking for short-term gain but seeing where he or she can 'give'. Our giving behaviour creates a relationship of trust and respect, and in the medium to long term we gain so much more than we would have had we decided to be the user or the manipulator. But the motivation to build a relationship is expressed in the interest we have in other people, and not because we think we might personally benefit – even in the long term. The benefits are a happy by-product of the relationship, not the prime motivating factor.

So networking is really about 'building' strong personal relationships. But how do we do this? As an exercise, think how you behave when you actually fancy someone and are meeting them for the first time. What do you do? Make a note of some of the things you do in that situation. As we look at our list we notice things like:

■ We make them the centre of our attention
■ We listen attentively
■ We show concern for their thoughts and feelings
■ We find out about them by asking questions

Well, it's just like that with networking too. Here are some key points that will help us develop strong relationships. They don't just relate to networking. They get to the heart of what we call our 'interpersonal skills'.

Keep an open mind

Keep as open-minded about people as we do about opportunities. Don't just share your time with people who have similar likes and interests to you. It is understandable that we do this. When we meet new people we try to find areas of common ground that will provide a basis for a better relationship. But if we seek out only these people, we shut out many more from our life.

Be interested in them

It's tempting to tell people all about ourselves because most of us like people to think good of us. But showing interest in others first sends out a signal that we care about them. Listening and questioning skills play an essential role here. Asking open 'who, what, why, where, when, how?' questions provides a useful basis for opening up conversation. But asking 'what do you think?' type questions shows that we value their thoughts, opinions and world-view.

But all this questioning goes only so far. If it becomes obvious that you are asking questions to see what you can get out of them, people will feel used. When you listen, show that you are actually listening. Body language plays an important part here, as does eye contact. Many readers will know that these skills get to the heart of what we call 'active listening'. But we can go one step further. By listening 'projectively' we try to get into the other person's world. We try to really understand. To do this we need to suspend our own opinions and prejudices and almost see ourselves as a blank canvas absorbing paint.

At work make yourself available, keep in touch and return calls to show that you are interested. Little things matter as much as the big ones.

Be genuine

People don't want you to like them just because you see a gold mine of opportunity in them. They want to know that you do care. Of course you can't force yourself to be genuine if you don't feel it. Some people are good at pretending. But most of us are not very good at hiding lack of interest.

Crawling all over people may benefit you in the short term, but if people see this they will ignore you when you need them.

I am here to help

Offering help to people makes them remember you. It makes them more inclined to help you when you need it – behaviour breeds behaviour. But do remember that your giving of help should be done because you want to, not because you have an expectation of a favour being returned. People, particularly in the workplace, will begin to see your relationship as an alliance.

Overcome shyness

Many people are shy about proactively meeting new people. We are afraid of what they might think. We say to ourselves, 'I might not have anything to say' or 'They might wonder what I am doing there.' And so we may shy away from making contact. There are confidence issues here (my earlier book *Positive Thinking, Positive Action* provides advice), but if you do want to meet people and find it uncomfortable to do so, it can be helpful to have a friend or colleague to introduce you and help you climb that first hurdle.

Give your best

Amid the short-termism that characterizes many relationships, there is one factor that shines through. If you're competent, capable and interested in people they will invest in you too and, in the medium to long term, relationships develop that are genuine and based in mutual benefit.

…And the result?

We notice what we call the 'network spiral effect' kicking in – the more people who feel we value them, the more they value us and we both benefit.

When people respect and value us they tell other people too and more opportunities come at us. Building great relationships requires an investment in people but, as with all great investments, we let them bubble away nicely and we reap the reward.

Valon's story – building relationships

I live in Kosovo and when I say that it immediately conjures up images of war, migration and lack of opportunity. I have to say that for a short period of time in our history this was true for many Kosovars. It was

1999 and the Serbian army had decided to occupy Kosovo. The true story of what happened in that period is still being told but many of us know the sort of things that went on. People still search for family and friends who disappeared, never to be found again. Houses were pulled down and infrastructure destroyed and it became impossible to lead anything closely resembling a normal life. In no time at all many people became refugees, escaping as quickly as they could to different parts of Europe.

Anyway I found myself as a refugee over the border in Albania with 10,000 others. They were putting up huge tents to give everyone shelter and it occurred to me that my skills may be of use. I am a qualified electrical engineer and I approached some of the workers there and told them what I could do. I had studied electronics back in Kosovo and I had worked with many colleagues on various electric projects in my homeland and in Albania. I immediately became centrally involved – I co-ordinated a team of people to get a power supply working. My countrymen and women were able to have some power supply so they could cook food. Of course at this time my efforts were all about survival and the survival of my fellow refugees and I wasn't paid. Someone asked why I was doing all this work for no money and I can honestly say that I was just glad to help my countrymen. I did this job without any expectation of any reward but I must confess my name did start to become well known – 10,000 people are likely to know who has provided them with power for heating and cooking when they had none before!

NATO decided to intervene and repel the Serb army and eventually Kosovars were able to return to Kosovo and I had to look for other opportunities. Someone had done an article in an Albanian newspaper about my work in the camp and I started to get work in Albania as an electrician because of it. I needed to earn some money! But the time soon came to return to my homeland and I started to do some work with an international organization called 'Samaritan's Purse' who were based in my hometown of Gjakova and I worked with them on a shelter programme that provided accommodation for 700 families. I organized all the logistics (I think my 'networking skills' really helped here) so that we could get all the food and non-food essentials into the area for families who badly needed them. I spent a year with them. I remember one of the really special times was when we managed to get shoeboxes of presents together for the children in the area at Christmas time. This is something Samaritan's Purse do throughout the world – over 400,000 children get Christmas presents thanks to them.

I suppose I did start to think about my 'people skills' at that time. I hope I can be described as 'nice'. I am open, or at least I try to be, but I am quite straight and to the point – I suppose 'nice but assertive' probably describes me accurately. And those were the skills I needed to get things done. At this time I started to get a bit restless – I needed new challenges. Because of my work in Gjakova a Swedish election official asked me to join him in his work on the democratization programme in the area. Without my work at the Samaritan's Purse I would not have got the opportunity. I really feel that my giving of myself was starting to pay me back (although I never had any expectation that it would) and I ended up working as an election specialist for three years – right up to 2005.

While all the work with Samaritan's Purse was going on, I was running a late-night restaurant – I had to earn a living! But one night we were listening to a radio show on the local station and I decided to phone in and try and join the discussion. Well, things started to happen and I got voted best contributor and was then invited to start my own show after testing out my material. There was no money in local radio in Kosovo then and I did a show for three years for no salary. But I loved it. We kept the show humorous but didn't shirk any of the big issues of the time – and there were a lot of political issues in Kosovo at that time as you can imagine!

Well, after a time I was asked to take the show on to television. I started my show on the newly formed but underfunded KTV and after three or four weeks it became the biggest TV show in Kosovo. I did two further TV series on KTV and two more series of shows on another channel – TV21 We did comedy sketches, interviews and formal interviews with prominent politicians. In the early days I wasn't paid. The reality is that, if I had wanted to be paid at the outset I wouldn't have had any TV show. What ended up happening was that after giving of myself for free, people started to give money to me and I became a very highly paid TV performer by Kosovo standards. The TV work continues – I am currently researching a 12-part serial which will go on air soon throughout the region.

I feel like I know just everybody in Kosovo. Certainly most people know me now because of my radio and TV work, but in truth I think I had a lot of contacts before that. When I go back 10 or 15 years I see that I spent a lot of time with people, helping them out. I have a political career ahead of me and I do seem to have a lot of support but I think that politics is for the future. Perhaps the relationships I have built in the last 15 years will help me but I certainly didn't build relationships for that reason. I am now an executive director of a new privately funded university in Kosovo – we have 1,100 students already and my networking and people skills are proving to be invaluable in getting finance. Many of our political figures are studying there (as am I) and I am getting them involved in the work of the university – particularly with raising funds and helping with the profile of it.

We have a very old Albanian saying:

Summer always comes once near your door. You must open the door.

I think I have opened many doors without having to force them open. I think if you apply the right attitude with people then they remember you. I think my life so far shows that.

◼ I want to be taken seriously!

We all want to be taken seriously but sometimes it can be a struggle to get people to see you that way. As we seek to take opportunities it can be incredibly frustrating when people don't see the capability in you that you see in yourself. Just imagine as you read some of the personal stories in this book if those people hadn't been taken seriously by others – they would not have got very far. In fact some of them had to work hard to convince others of their capabilities.

Here are some simple steps that can help. First, seek to confirm if your perception is accurate.

Someone isn't taking me seriously and it's holding me back

It may be that in the short term someone is convinced of our capability and competence and gives us a break. Or it may be that our previous track record provides evidence that we are good at what we do and that we have experience. But, as they say, people buy people and we often find ourselves having to prove ourselves or to win the trust of others. This can be very frustrating when, for example, we have proved what we can do in one job and then have to start again in another. Or when a new manager comes into our company and doesn't know what we can do. Sometimes we have to start all over again. The joy of building relationships across networks over many years is that people often help us when we need them to but life isn't always that simple. What will decide whether your relationship becomes a stronger one is the amount that you choose to put in.

We need good relationships with other people to get on. But other people may not take us seriously (or so we believe) and we find our efforts to spot and take opportunities stall early. So if we feel that others don't take us seriously, how can we be sure that we are not mistaken? Ask yourself:

1 Are you being selective in what you are seeing and hearing? If we believe that people see us in a particular way we look out for signs that confirm our view and ignore the signals that might challenge that point of view.

2 Are you guilty of compromising your behaviour because you believe that a person doesn't take you seriously? If we think that someone sees us in a particular way we tend to behave according to that stereotype OR we overcompensate in our behaviour, perhaps becoming aggressive or passive. In other words we create our own reality through our own behaviour. If we are uncomfortable because of this, then we may display signs of discomfort to the other person.

3 Was there a single event that may have triggered this? Can you pinpoint a time or place that might have caused the other person to think this way? For example, you might be going to the bank manager to raise money for something. If your previous record makes it difficult for the bank manager to take your request seriously then you will have to work harder to prove you are trustworthy.

Or was there a time when someone needed your help and you were unable to give it?

4 Could this just be a reflection of their personal insecurities? Do they lack self-esteem? Could they see you as a threat? Are you much younger?

So we can ask ourselves these questions to help us decide if there is any truth in our fears about not being taken seriously. If your fears are proved correct, here are three things you can do to deal with the situation – one is a short-term solution, while the others require a commitment of time.

1 Ask directly

You can ask them if this is true. Before you do this you need to have concrete examples of where their behaviour with you leads you to believe that this is the case – a vague 'I don't think you like me very much' isn't helpful. Your style needs to be assertive – honest, open, in control, confident – but not aggressive. And make sure that you don't do all the talking – your style should be geared to opening up the other person. Avoid bombarding the other person with a verbal download of all your grievances.

2 Why should they take you seriously?

You may have to accept that while you are the centre of your own world you are not the centre of theirs. Why should they take you seriously? You may need to invest some time and earn their respect – to build up your credibility in their eyes – rather than expecting it right away. The days are gone when respect was automatically granted because of status or because of the roles we filled in society. Respect has to be earned – particularly perhaps among the younger generation.

3 Invest some time in the person

Commit to building a stronger relationship over time. Becoming a better listener is one skill that you can develop – and remember to use the person's name when you talk to them. We all like the sound of our own name. People are much more interested in us if we are genuinely interested in them. As time passes things will improve and if the relationship strengthens sufficiently new opportunities will open up. If they see that you take them seriously (and aren't sycophantic) then they will begin to see you in a more serious light too.

Remember too the suggestions given in the earlier part of the section.

Procrastination is like an elastic band that stretches into the future and brings the regretful 'if only' statement nearer to our lips.

12
Getting motivated

- ❏ Taking steps
- ❏ What's right for you…
- ❏ …may not be right for me!
- ❏ Trying too hard – Barry's story

This is the final chapter. I have left it until last because the indivisible truth about going for opportunities is that it requires us to be motivated to do so. This may seem obvious but many times we will hear someone say, 'I never got the opportunities' or 'Nothing ever happens to me' and we notice that in many instances the people who say these things never proactively did anything about it.

■ Taking steps

Many of us spot opportunities. Where we stall is in taking the next steps to making the most of the opportunities we have identified. We are quite good at putting things off, so what does it take to push us into taking the steps to getting motivated? Our motivation becomes really important when we need to make good decisions (Stage 3) and when we take action (Stage 4). Taking opportunities can mean major change. What are the steps to getting motivated to take these major changes?

There are several reasons why we put off making major changes. They include:

■ Past failures

Where we think we have failed in the past (even if our perception is inaccurate) we can find ourselves disinclined to try again for fear of repeating the experience. Or if we feel that God is constantly unzipping the clouds over our lives, we begin to feel that nothing we do can change things for the better.

■ Fear of the unknown

T-Mobile, the mobile phone network provider, ran a campaign promoting their easy-to-follow bills with a strap line: 'If only life were this predictable.' Well, thank goodness life isn't predictable. There would be little stimulation if that were the case and we would soon wither and die.

Even though we need this unpredictability it can scare us, and this fear can stop us venturing into the unknown.

■ I'm comfortable

Some of us psychologically melt into the background at an alarmingly young age. Others enjoy a highly proactive life from the beginning right to the end. If we feel too comfortable we may be happy surrounded in psychological soft furnishings.

■ Boredom

There is a paradox here that says that when we are bored and should in theory crave excitement we find ourselves sliding down the apathy spiral.

■ What's easiest?

Let's face it, taking opportunities requires effort. And it is often easier to do something that gives instant gratification than put in the effort to seek longer-term and deeper gratification.

OK, so what are the steps?

Pleasure and pain

Psychologists often talk of the pleasure and pain associated with motivation. Rather than seeing the pain associated with particular positive actions and using it as an excuse not to put in the effort, look at the pain involved if you don't take the necessary actions. For example, if deep down you know that the threat of redundancies hangs over where you work, logic says that you should start looking around for a new job right away. This requires effort ('the pain'). But imagine what the pain might be if you respond only when you have been made redundant.

We might see the instant pleasure in spending five nights a week in front of the television set, but imagine the real long-term pleasure we might get if we applied ourselves on one or two of those nights to something that invested in our longer-term fulfilment.

We can build on this future pleasure thinking. When we make changes in our lives many of us naturally think of the loss. We can combat this by thinking what we might gain – the pleasure – of taking particular actions.

Nearly all change involves loss, but if we never changed then the real loser would be our quality of life.

Looking back from the future
This topic is a running theme throughout the book and it bears repeating. How might we feel in 20 years' time – what regrets might we have – if we didn't do the things we want to do now but are struggling to motivate ourselves for?

You are not going to live for ever
There is nothing like becoming aware of our own mortality to make us want to maximize the potential of each day. You are not immortal – even though we all like to believe that we are the one person who is. Understand this and you may find yourself energized to reach out at the things you were previously putting off. If you don't do it now, when exactly do you propose to do it?

Change for positive reasons
We often change things in our life (or not!) because of the dissatisfaction we have with our current circumstances. While this is a valid reason, it is probably not a prime motivating factor in itself. The bigger motivation – the building up of a kind of inner fire – comes from the excitement we generate about our future. For example, changing jobs because of dissatisfaction with the current one may provide some motivation. We all know people who complain about their jobs but 12 months on they still work at the same place. Far better to change jobs because you are excited about the new one or the potential of a new one rather than disillusionment with the old one.

Keep curious
Keep stimulating yourself by keeping curious and by keeping on the lookout for new experiences. Some say that we lose our capacity to be curious as we get older. We don't lose our capacity to be curious. What really happens is that we lose the *desire* to be curious. This happens because we become naturalized by surroundings and institutionalized by our jobs. We begin to see no other way and as a result don't entertain the possibility of a life that

continues to probe, ask questions and which is stimulated by new things.

Maintaining curiosity is one of the keys to longevity. And curiosity is one of the keys to finding new opportunities. We find that pursuing a new avenue of possibility opens up a web of opportunity.

Whole...Heart...Head...Ness

We commit ourselves best to change when we appeal to both the emotional and rational sides of ourselves. What I call the 'Whole...Heart...Head' approach. If we can find a combination of rational reasons (new opportunities, financial benefits and so on) AND emotional reasons (excitement at the unknown, for example) we increase the chances that we will go for it. Make a list of the rational and emotional reasons for wanting to change.

Turn a negative into a positive

Don't feel guilty about your negative thoughts when you are trying to get motivated. Your negative thoughts can be used to provide an injection of rational thinking, realistic thinking. Getting motivated means thinking positively, but thinking positively is not about chanting quasi-religious mantras while straddling fluffy white clouds. Part of thinking positively requires us to see things as they really are. Pessimistic thoughts about opportunity and change are fine because we can use them to work through the challenges in our mind in advance. When the challenges hit us we say to ourselves, 'I recognize this, and I have a plan to deal with it.'

Every problem has a solution

In fact every problem has more than one solution. Even when we've got ourselves motivated to take up a new opportunity we can find ourselves stalling as soon as we hit the first problem. Life rarely rolls out the red carpet for us.

Commitment

Ultimately, however, we have to commit to two things. First, make a commitment to get more involved in life and the opportunities will open up for you. Second, commitment to change requires personal responsibility. Pointing the finger at other people, your employer and so on, can go on for ever. Eventually the biggest finger points back at you and says: 'What are YOU going to do about it then?'

What do you want to achieve?

The point about your motivation to do something may well depend on how much you want to achieve something. The desire to achieve exists within all of us but the motivation to achieve provides an important starting point in building a more fulfilling life. However, the very word 'achievement' will mean different things to different people and it is important always to ask why you are doing something before taking up a new opportunity. What achievement need might you be fulfilling?

Much research has been put into the achievement needs that we have and the results show that they fall into a number of categories:

1 Money.
2 Because we need to compete – and win!
3 To show ourselves up well to our peer group.
4 Because we want to do it by ourselves and prove we can.
5 Because we want to succeed through hard work.
6 To make our family proud of us.
7 To receive the approval of experts in our field.
8 To get a sense of pride when we are able to help people.

You may be able to add some others. This all goes back to the reasons we identified earlier (the '4 Rs', page 72). Ask:

■ Which need will this opportunity fulfil in me?

■ Am I doing it for the money and/or peer group approval?

■ Am I doing it because I want my family to be proud of me?

■ Am I doing it to prove to myself that I can?

These are important questions to ask because we can then identify the possible rewards we might get. We fully engage only when we believe there is something in it for us (I exclude spontaneous altruistic acts of great courage where we act almost on impulse). So to return to the '4 Rs' – what are the 'rewards' for me?

■ What's right for you...

When two people do the same thing it is not the same thing.
Old proverb

Remember that old chestnut, 'If I were you...' The whole process of making decisions and then worrying if you have made the right one can lead to our emotions feeling like they are being thrown around inside a washing machine. The link between making the decision and the next critical phase when we act on that decision will be subjected to all sorts of pressures both internal and external. For example, some of those critical decisions we may make in our life – moving to a new area, changing job or even less significant personal choices like buying a new car – are tough enough in themselves but the whole process becomes tougher when we have others offering their opinion.

That is of course their right but you also have the right to take the course of action that is right for you. When others subject our life choices to critique they may have our best interests at heart but too often it may be because they are transposing their own personal wishes on our own lives. A cynical view maybe, and perhaps a little unfair at times, but it is always a valuable exercise to go back to the original reason you thought that this opportunity was significant for you. If those reasons are still valid and the heartfelt desire for change still burns, then why not?

When listening to opinions, do remember that opinions are just that – they are not facts. Advice is helpful but rarely are two situations identical and never are two people the same.

These 'push-pull' factors (thoughts, feelings and opinions) will dance in the mind all the time and will create the emotional rollercoaster that changes in our life create. If we expect there to be few we may be thinking unrealistically. Consider what it must be like to be one of the estimated 45 million refugees in the world at present. The factors pulling you back to your original home must be very strong – a lifetime of investment in laying personal roots, cultural identification and not least strong family ties. And yet many in that situation will still choose to seek out opportunities in new surroundings where the risks will be higher but where the opportunities will be greater – the post-hurricane Katrina fallout prompted many to seek opportunity elsewhere. The awareness of what is being left behind is likely to be strong but the excitement at what lies ahead is stronger.

And besides, if we find ourselves being pulled backed to the 'soft furnishings' of our current circumstances, perhaps we didn't want to make the most of the opportunity we had identified in the first place.

When making decisions to go for new opportunities, and when under pressure from others, try to remember the following factors:

■ Ask: Why did I want to do this in the first place? Are my reasons still strong?

■ Always remember how this will benefit you directly before you take account of others' opinions.

■ Listen to advice but critically analyse it: is it contaminated by that person's own opinions, prejudices, jealousy or lack of appreciation as to why you want to make the change?

■ There is unfortunately a group of people who seem to take pleasure in the apparent failure of others, or in saying 'I told you so' when we fail to meet challenges. These are usually people who have the time to think proactively about other people's lives but seem to have no time to do something proactive with their own.

Pursuing opportunities for somebody else's emotional benefit is counter-productive. Parents, for example, can provide wonderful emotional support and guidance but can also transpose their own wishes and desires on to their children. Your life is not your parent's life. And neither is it anybody else's.

Things will happen for you in your new circumstances that you cannot plan for. Tell yourself that surprises and unplanned events do not mean that you made the wrong decision. They are merely tests for you to prove to yourself and the rest of the world that you made the right one!

■ …may not be right for me!

Part of the process of getting motivated involves understanding the kind of person you are, matched with the kind of opportunity you are looking for. In different situations different approaches will be needed. For example in 'Fruit picking' (pages 146–153) we look at two examples of opportunities that were there for a very short time and therefore needed to be grasped. And we do have to say that some people aren't temperamentally suited to this kind of rapid change – although it is remarkable how quickly we can move when we have to, even if we aren't used to the high-octane lifestyle. However, there are other kinds of opportunities that really don't go away – opportunities that can be taken at our choosing or which deserve a commitment of time.

Trying too hard

Someone once said that slowing down can be important because we need to allow things time to catch up with us. Think about the salesperson who is excited about a prospective sale and pushes too hard. Or the sportsperson who gets an injury and, in their excitement to get back on the pitch, comes back too soon and gets injured again. Sometimes we can try too hard.

Trying too hard – Barry's story (apocryphal)

I had reached the age of 38 and although I've had relationships with women I haven't really had a relationship that lasted for any length of time. I looked enviously at some of my friends who had lasting relationships. And of course they were telling me how lucky I was! I suppose I had lots of opportunities to form relationships as we all do but I tended in hindsight, to jump in and say, 'This is the one' and it would finish almost before the relationship started. I started to behave unnaturally in my concern to make this work. Things like this can knock your confidence. You start thinking that you are unattractive or have some deeply unappealing personality trait that puts people off.

One of the joys of being single is that you have plenty of time to think about yourself. This can be a bad thing sometimes – too much self-reflection is not healthy. But as I started to think about things I started to realize that I'm really a happy person. I enjoy my life but I think I just wanted someone to share it with. At that point I decided that I was actually almost trying to make myself unhappy by forcing myself to do something that I didn't really need to.

Sometimes I think we just try a bit too hard to get what we want, or what we think we want, in life. I learnt that sometimes it can pay to slow down a little – to do things that are right for the kind of person you are.

You know where my story is going don't you? As soon as I stopped trying too hard I met someone. I didn't even realize it at the time. It just sort of happened. Will it last? Well it's lasted longer than most! And I'm being myself. I've learnt that when I'm natural people appreciate me for what I am. People tend to see through you when you pretend to be something that you are not. I am not one of these people who lives in a whirlwind of energy and I suppose the way I form relationships was no exception. I learnt that we get opportunities all the time. Sometimes we do need to take them quickly. But sometimes, particularly with opportunities that are there all the time we don't need to be frenetic. With this relationship I learnt that sometimes it is OK to take it slowly, to let things build.

If this book is the breakfast of opportunity,
then you can live the
morning snack, lunch,
high tea, tea, dinner
and supper of fulfilment.
Eat well, my friends.

Conclusion
A checklist of handy hints

❑ A mental tool-kit

❑ Shine like the stars – where do you want to get to?

❑ And finally…are you curious enough?

In this final section we provide reminders of some of the key points from the book in 'bite-size' form. We begin with a tool-kit for the OST. We follow that with a reminder of some of the thought processes and actions that will help us reach our 'stellar' aspirations and finally we provide a checklist of mindsets that act as a catalyst for the opportunity spotter – these mindsets are based around being curious. This curiosity is a theme we will work with in the follow on book to this one.

■ A mental tool-kit

So to start here are a few tips to help us as we go through a life of spotting and taking opportunities. Use them as a handy little mental tool-kit.

■ **A flexible mind works best.** No two situations are the same. What worked once may not work the next time. Ask if there is another way of doing this. Ask if there is another way of seeing the problem.

■ **Action and exploration breed opportunity.** Keep ahead by looking rather than waiting.

■ **Use the crystal ball.** We often don't see opportunities that are staring at us. Take control by pre-empting your future of opportunity rather than the future controlling you.

■ **Be open to spontaneity.** The most enjoyable opportunities often live best in spontaneity. This book has a bias towards the planned and well thought out spotting and taking of opportunities but many will arrive 'in the moment'. We cannot plan for spontaneity but we can learn to enjoy the impulsive and spontaneous rather than be frightened by it.

■ **Access first-time experiences.** Remember that quote: 'When was the last time you did something for the first time?' It's amazing how taking opportunities acts as the spark that generates even more of them. Sometimes we have to keep the lid on when so much comes at us!

■ **Be prepared.** The luckiest people tend to be those who are prepared for opportunities. The luck doesn't really exist – our readiness for the opportunity creates the luck for us.

■ **Use uncertainty and ambiguity.** Life is full of uncertainty and ambiguity, which often create problems for us. Can you learn to see the problem as opportunity?

■ Shine like the stars – where do you want to get to?

We all have ambitions. And our capacity both to spot and take opportunities gets to the heart of us meeting those ambitions. Spotting and taking opportunities provides the bridge between the dream and the reality. So here are some 'stellar' thoughts that remind us how we can start to build that bridge.

S – Star

The limits we place on our capacity to spot opportunities are restricted only by the breadth of our ambitions in life. If we really want to aim for the stars we are more likely to spot the opportunity that will take us there. A limited desire for personal fulfilment will mean that we see less opportunity around us. The choice is yours. How much do you really want personal fulfilment?

T – Time

Arrive early. It is easy to see opportunities when they are gone. It is easy to see a problem when it is looking straight at us. And if things are going well for us in our career or in our business we can think that the good times will last forever. But picking your moment to go for new opportunities is key here. Take on the new challenge at the moment when you chose and not when the moment chooses you.

E – Energizing

Remember Kath Joy's quote when asked, 'Why do you want to take on this new challenge?' Her reply was simple: 'Because I want that feeling of being alive.'

L – Life before death

With our time limited, it's amazing how much of it we waste. When we realize that our time is shorter than we imagined, we really start to appreciate and access the things that give us a sense of enjoyment and fulfilment. Knowing when to rest and recharge is important. But sitting on the metaphorical sofa for your whole life will not get you that 'feeling of being alive'.

L – Looking back

Remember the quote right at the beginning of the book? What would you like to say about your life at the end of it? To say that you 'had a go?' Or to have regrets that you didn't?

A – Attitude

The great freedom we have is to be able to choose our attitude in any given situation. No matter how big the problem, no matter how grave the situation, we can still choose the attitude we take – remember Ronald Searle's example (page 18). That positive attitude will help us knock down the wall that separates us from opportunity rather than making the wall even higher.

R – Rewards

We go for the new opportunity only if we believe that there will be rewards for us. The rewards may be intangible (a stronger sense of personal fulfilment) or they may be explicit (for 10 per cent growth in our business turnover next year). Whatever the perceived return, it can be highly motivating to believe that personal benefit will come from taking the opportunity.

■ And finally…are you curious enough?

So how much do you see around you? How interested are you in what's around you? Did you ever look through the lens of a telescope and find yourself asking endless questions about worlds beyond ours? Did you ever ask yourself, 'I wonder what would happen if I did this?' and then go and do it? Did you ever read a newspaper that was different from your regular one because you wanted to see how others might see the world? Do you like to spend a little bit of your day living in your imagination?

Curiosity is the energizer of the opportunity spotter! If you can learn to embrace and enjoy some the following things you are well on the way to being that great opportunity spotter. We can all do it – if we believe we can.

■ **The challenge** – because we want to know what we are capable of.

■ **The childishness** – children find reasons why things can be done before they find reasons why they cannot. Can you use child-like thinking processes to inspire your own curiosity?

■ **The confusion** – anyone who isn't confused isn't thinking straight. Making sense of the confusion – asking why things are the way they are – feeds the curious mind.

■ **The invention** – keeping our eyes open to the possibility of new ways of doing things keeps us alive to the possibility of creating something new.

■ **The inspiration** – what do you do when you have those eureka moments. Ignore them or write them down and explore further?

■ **The absurdity** – today's absurdity is tomorrow's normality. Don't dismiss that which you find absurd. To someone else it may be entirely normal. Can you laugh and enjoy the absurd rather than feel threatened by it?

■ **The humour** – the person who can laugh and maintain a sense of perspective is the one who will be open-minded and inspired by the new and intriguing.

■ **The mystery** – sometimes there are questions that just don't seem to have an answer. Are you curious enough to try and find out?

■ **Contradiction** – are you interested in exploring the reasons why the world seems full of contradictions or do you ignore them?

Ask the 'who, why, what, where, when, how?' questions to maintain curiosity. Out of the world of curiosity comes a raft of possibilities. When we realize what is possible we start to believe opportunity does indeed knock for us if we are prepared to be curious. The next step is to open the door and let it in. Life is much more fulfilling and fun if we chose to embrace the opportunities that exist for us rather than ignoring them. It is a simple choice to make.

> *Afoot and light-hearted I take to the open road*
> *Healthy, free, the world before me*
> *The long brown path before me leading wherever I choose*

Walt Whitman, *'Song of the Open Road'*

References

Books

I referenced material from the following books:

Barker, Joel, *The Business of Discovering the Future*, Harper Business, 1992

Brown, Mark, *The Dinosaur Strain*, ICE Books, 1993

Handy, Charles, *Beyond Certainty* Hutchinson, 1995

Handy, Charles, *The Empty Raincoat*, Hutchinson, 1994

Laing, R. D., *The Politics of Experience*, Penguin, 1974

Miller, Douglas, *Positive Thinking, Positive Action*, BBC Books, 2005

Vernon, M. D., *The Psychology of Perception*, Pelican, 1962

von Oech, Roger, *A Kick in the Seat of the Pants,* HarperCollins, 1986

Warner, Jon, *The Networking Pocketbook*, Management Pocketbooks, 1999

Wiseman, Richard, *Did You Spot The Gorilla?*, Arrow Books, 2004

Websites

www.creativethink.com – Roger Von Oech's personal website

www.iceeurope.com – Mark Brown's personal website

www.about.movies.com – quote from Cameron Diaz

■ Newspapers

These newspaper articles inspired me to write about the following:

'Anne and Doug Perkins – Specsavers', *Sunday Times*, 10 July 2005

'Woodworm – Freddie Flintoff', *Independent*, 6 September 2005

'Dave Pearson – BT Futurologist', *Observer*, 22 May 2005

'Apathy – The Eighth Deadly Sin', *Metro*, 1 September 2004

'The Fruits of Global Warming', *Independent*, 1 August 2005

Acknowledgements

I would like to acknowledge the work of the following in developing Part One of this book – Mark Brown, Roger von Oech, Joel Barker and Charles Handy. Some of their writings are referenced in the bibliography, as are their personal websites. I would also like to thank those whose real-life experiences have added a strong sense of realism to the theory presented in Part Two of the book.

I would like to thank Emma Shackleton, the commissioning editor at BBC Active, who continues to support my ideas for new topics. I hope that my books justify the invaluable backing she gives to me. Can I also express a really heartfelt thank you to Christine King, who has copy-edited this book.

My personal thanks also to baby chimp, the pet monkey and the hen. Also to Suba, Nacao Zumbi, Jan Garbarek, Lambchop, Anthony and the Johnsons and Pharaoh Sanders who provided the glorious soundtrack as I wrote the book.

I welcome comments, questions and great stories from readers. You can contact me at: doug@dougmiller.demon.co.uk